THE TOP 2%

HOW TO BECOME THE
HIGHEST-PAID, HIGHEST-PROFILE
PERSON IN YOUR INDUSTRY

Nightingale-Conant
and The Staff of Entrepreneur Media, Inc.

Entrepreneur Press®

Entrepreneur Press, Publisher
Cover Design: Andrew Welyczko
Production and Composition: Eliot House Productions

This publication is designed to provide accurate and authoritative information
in regard to the subject matter covered. It is sold with the understanding that
the publisher is not engaged in rendering legal, accounting, or other professional
services. If legal advice or other expert assistance is required, the services of a
competent professional person should be sought.

Entrepreneur Press® is a registered trademark of Entrepreneur Media, Inc.

An application to register this book for cataloging has been submitted to the
Library of Congress.

ISBN 978-1-64201-111-1 (paperback) | ISBN 978-1-61308-434-2 (ebook)

Printed in the United States of America

25 24 23 22   10 9 8 7 6 5 4 3 2 1

CONTENTS

INTRODUCTION

In 1956, Earl Nightingale wrote and recorded a message that he called *The Strangest Secret*. In a short period of time, without advertising or marketing, more than a million copies had been sold. In fact, *The Strangest Secret* earned a gold record. It's the only gold record ever achieved for the spoken word.

One of the people who heard *The Strangest Secret* was Lloyd Conant, the owner of a Chicago printing and direct-response company. Lloyd contacted Earl and the two became fast friends. Their common bond? Their shared values of success.

In 1960, Earl Nightingale and Lloyd Conant formed the Nightingale-Conant corporation so they could share those values with the world. They started with the now-classic success program *Lead the Field. Lead the Field* became a bestseller as well, touching the lives of more than a million people.

Since then, Nightingale-Conant has featured the wisdom and success principles of hundreds of individuals who are at the top of virtually every industry.

After 50 years of teaching success, Nightingale Learning Systems has gathered the common bonds and shared values of those individuals who occupy the rarest positions in their industries—the top 2%.

Who better to create a strategy about becoming the highest-paid, highest-profile person in your industry than the company that was founded on those values and who has featured hundreds of authors who are *in* the top 2% of their fields? And who better to partner with to bring this timeless content to a new audience than Entrepreneur Press? For over 40 years, Entrepreneur has been the voice of authority on entrepreneurship and success. Now these two powerhouse brands team up to share their insight with you.

With *The Top 2%*, our intention is to follow in Nightingale-Conant's founder's footsteps and his classic *Lead the Field* program by providing the latest research on what it takes to reach the top in any industry. It is our hope that this book achieves the same legendary status and provides the road map for the next generation of achievers— starting with you.

SUCCESS ISN'T MAGIC

Think about the most successful people you have read about. People like Steve Jobs, Warren Buffet, Shonda Rimes, Vera Wang, Bill and Melinda Gates, and Oprah Winfrey. Did their success happen because of random events? Is Warren Buffet the Oracle of Omaha because of luck? Is Oprah's success story a fluke? Are they just lucky people who happened to be at the right places at the right times?

No. Their success is based on far more than random events or luck. They have followed a pattern of attitudes and behaviors that directly led to their success. And this book will share stories of other people who've done the same thing.

Both Nightingale-Conant and Entrepreneur have had the honor and pleasure of working with some of the most successful people in just about every industry. Nightingale-Conant has featured authors from the fields of medicine and science, nutrition and health, wealth building and money management, sales and marketing, metaphysics and spirituality, public speaking and business skills, and many others. In addition, Nightingale-Conant has also created branded programs through Nightingale Learning Systems: *The Power of Passive Income, The FlexBrain Method, The Richest Man in Babylon,* and *Focused Mind, Powerful Mind.* Likewise, the team at Entrepreneur has written about, interviewed, and collaborated with the some of the most successful thought leaders and influencers in the small-business and entrepreneurship spaces, from Brian Tracy and Dan S. Kennedy to Gary Vaynerchuck and Daymond John.

You might be wondering, "Why the 2%? Most leaders and success experts look only at the top 5%. What's so special about the 2%?"

The fact is, there is a dramatic difference in achievement and wellness between the people who are in the top 2% and those who are in the top 5%. According to *The Wall Street Journal,* over 5 million people moved from the top 5% in wealth to the top 1% in wealth in the last two decades. The incomes of the top earners in the U.S. are growing faster than the incomes of any other segment of the population.

Even when you're not talking about money, it's still better to be in the top 2% than the top 5%. Wouldn't you rather be in the top 2% of healthy people? The top 2% of happy people? Have relationships that are better than 98% of everyone else's?

The days when being in the top 5% was good enough are gone. We live in a global village with, frankly, a bigger pool of talented, motivated people who are competing against each other. When you apply the ideas and techniques you learn in this book, you'll be poised to be in the top 2% of any area you choose to succeed in. A core set of attitudes and behaviors are common among those who are the top 2% in every industry. We've figured out the formula, and we're going to share it with you.

You see, the fact is, the top 2% set the trends in every industry. They set the trends by imagining and dreaming things that didn't exist and then doing what it took to make it happen. Whether you're in business, entertainment, sports, politics, or some other industry, if you're in the top 2%, you have the power and influence to make things happen.

WHAT TO EXPECT IN THIS BOOK

Before we get any further, let's talk about how this book is structured. The editors at Nightingale Learning Systems spent months researching through their library and identified 17 principles of success that were common among all their top authors. Regardless of whether you're listening to Anthony Robbins, Marc David, John Cummuta, or Zig Ziglar, these principles are common to all of them.

Next, they arranged the principles into a model that is represented by the shape of a star. Each of the points of the star represents one area of success. The letters in the word *STARS* stand for the qualities we identified. So, the S stands for *Sense of Purpose*. The T stands for *Traits*. The A is for *Attitudes*. The R stands for *Rapport with Others*. And the last S stands for *Skills*. We'll talk about each one of these and give you examples of people in the top 2% who've mastered these qualities as well as some tips and strategies so that you can master them, too.

The most important quality that runs through all 17 principles is an overarching sense of purpose. We'll talk about what that is and how you can develop your own Overarching Sense of Purpose. Along the way, we'll provide tips and advice from the staff of Entrepreneur to help bring these concepts to life.

REACH FOR THE STARS

Are you ready to rocket to the STARS? Let's start with a little assessment quiz. It's called "How Close Are You to the STARS?" and it asks 18 true-or-false questions. Take a look at them in Figure I–1 on page xiii and see how close you are:

FIGURE I-1. How Close Are You to the STARS?

	True	False
1. I know my life's purpose.		
2. There is something that I feel incredibly passionate about.		
3. I consider myself to be an entrepreneur even if I have a "regular job."		
4. I've got a good self-image.		
5. I'm one of the most energetic people I know.		
6. My physical health is excellent.		
7. I enjoy learning new things all the time.		
8. Even though I have goals for the future, I'm happy now.		
9. I've got good self-discipline.		
10. I am thinking about the legacy I'm going to leave my friends and family after I'm gone.		
11. People tell me I'm a good communicator.		
12. I focus on serving others as much as possible.		
13. I have meaningful relationships.		
14. I consider myself to be a great negotiator.		
15. I've got goals for the major areas of my life.		
16. I'm good at managing my time and getting things done.		
17. I consider myself an excellent money manager.		
18. I can come up with creative solutions to problems.		

Of course, the STARS answers to all these questions are true. But don't worry if you're not there yet. We'll teach you what you need to know so you can be among the STARS as well.

And remember, following your dreams is worthwhile. Your dreams are like the stars you see in the night sky. You may never touch them, but if you follow them, they will lead you to your destiny.

In the first chapter, we'll get into the most important quality that is common to all the STARS in the top 2%: an overarching sense of purpose.

THE TOP QUALITY OF THE TOP 2%

An Overarching Sense of Purpose

What's the thing that causes triathletes to get up in the middle of the night to exercise? What's the thing that causes entrepreneurs to pour their money, heart, soul, and energy into their product or business? What's the one thing that can cause a person to donate blood out of their own body to someone else? It's an overarching sense of purpose. Triathletes do it because they want to win. Entrepreneurs do it because they passionately believe in their product or service. Blood donors do it because they know that donating blood saves lives. People are willing to endure incredible pain, hardship, and sacrifice if they have a deep sense of purpose.

By purpose, we aren't talking about an objective or something that you're striving for. As Ken Blanchard put it, "Purpose is something bigger. It is the picture you have of yourself—the kind of person you want to be or the kind of life you want to lead."

This is going to be an exciting chapter because we're going to talk about something that is, in essence, the umbrella that encompasses all the other qualities. It's at the very top of the STARS model because it's the thing that makes you reach higher and higher.

WORK TO LIVE—DON'T LIVE TO WORK

Motivational speaker Les Brown tells a story of what motivated him to find his purpose. He says, "I remember coming from a friend of mine's funeral, and I was reflecting on how much time I had left. I went for walk in the park, thinking about this guy whose life was so promising. He wasn't an old guy—he was quite young, in fact—and I thought about all the things he said he was going to do and he never got a chance to do those things. I started thinking about my own life and how much time I had left to do the things that I would like to do, and, at that time, I wasn't sure what my life's purpose was. I wasn't sure about it at that time. I thought about it quite a lot. I had some ideas, but I wasn't convinced. I don't think I felt worthy. I didn't believe it could be *me* that was to do this work I'm doing right now. I say to you that if you began to make a conscious effort to find out what it is that you are supposed to do, I say that it can *literally save your life*. It can literally save your life."

Do you think Les Brown is exaggerating when he says that finding your life's purpose can literally save your life? It's not an exaggeration. Dr. Larry Dossey, who wrote a book called *Recovering the Soul* (Bantam, 1989), said that human beings are the only living species that have achieved the dubious distinction of dying or having a stroke or heart attack on a certain day. If you ask most people, "What causes heart attacks?" Most people would talk about things like smoking, high blood pressure, obesity, and things like that. Of course, all those things are contributing factors, but did you know that more heart attacks take place in this country on Monday morning between 8 and 9 A.M. than any other time of the day or week? How can smoking or obesity cause a heart attack to happen at a specific time of day?

According to recent studies, 85 percent of the American public are going to jobs that they hate or do not challenge them. People get sick thinking about going to work. If they're not living on purpose, they might smoke or overeat to fill the void. They might get high blood pressure or other stress-related illnesses because they're not guided by a sense of purpose, and they don't have the peace that comes with it.

Think about it this way. When you go to a job that isn't part of an overarching sense of purpose, it feels like going to a movie where you've already seen the end. You know what the outcome is going to be. You can't get excited about experiencing that movie again. Contrast this with where you're going to a job and you have a strong sense that what you do matters. It doesn't even have to be brain surgery. You could be the guy that puts the paper clips inside the paper clip box. But if you have a sense of purpose and meaning about it, you're not going to be the one dropping dead of a heart attack on Monday morning.

Your life is worth finding out what it is you are supposed to do.

How much time do you spend working on you? How much time do you spend every day working on your dream? In the last 90 days, how many books have you read? In the last year, what new skill or knowledge have you acquired? What kind of investment have you made in you? Think about what you have done or can do in the future to work on YOU. Use the space provided in Figure 1–1 on page 4 to record your thoughts.

WHY YOU NEED A PURPOSE

OK, so we've talked about what having a sense of purpose can do for you at work. What are some other benefits of having a sense of purpose? Here are nine direct benefits of having an overarching sense of purpose. Some of these might surprise you:

1. *Reduced risk of getting Alzheimer's disease.* Individuals with a sense of purpose at the start of the study were less likely to develop Alzheimer's over the course of the study. In fact, it was shown that people with the lowest sense of purpose in life were more

FIGURE 1-1. Working on Myself

What I Do to Work on Myself

_____

_____

_____

_____

_____

_____

_____

_____

What I Want to Do in the Future to Work on Myself

_____

_____

_____

_____

_____

_____

_____

_____

than twice as likely to develop Alzheimer's than those with the highest sense of purpose.

2. *Stress reduction.* If you have a sense of purpose, you're going to experience a lowered perception of stress. In other words, if you've got two people in prison, but one of them feels there is a higher purpose to her imprisonment and the other feels that she's a victim of circumstance, the one with an overarching sense of purpose will have less stress.

3. *Fewer mistakes in life.* If you've got a sense of purpose, you're going to make fewer mistakes. Sure, even people who have a sense of purpose take risks and make mistakes. But if you know WHY you're doing something, you're less likely to make a mistake than someone who is randomly going from one thing to another.

4. *More resilient.* People who have a strong sense of purpose are more resilient and bounce back from adversity. Think about the people who lose weight. Pretty much everyone who's lost a significant amount of weight fell off the wagon once or twice. But the person who is losing weight because they realize that their life purpose is to help others lose weight or to live long enough to walk their daughter down the aisle is going to get right back on track. The one who doesn't have a purpose is going to have a harder time bouncing back.

5. *Better ability to say "no."* Think about it. If you know what your purpose is, then you know what your purpose ISN'T. And it becomes easier to say no to things that aren't part of your life's purpose.

6. *No longer need to "keep up with the Joneses."* This is an important one. When you know your life's purpose, you stop comparing yourself to other people who have a different purpose. It doesn't matter what kinds of things other people have or don't have, or what they do with their time. You know what you're doing and that's all that matters to you.

7. *Better relationships.* When you are living your life with a sense of purpose, you naturally attract other people who share that purpose.

Your relationships become more congruent and purpose filled. You stop wanting to spend time with people who don't support your purpose.

8. *Better money management.* This might surprise you. What does life purpose have to do with money management? If you know your life's purpose, you're not trying to fill that void with things. You spend your resources in ways that matter to you. For example, if your life's purpose is about saving the Earth, then your money is going to be spent on things that are eco-friendly. You might not be spending LESS money, but you'll be managing your money better and thinking about *how* you spend your money.

9. *Improved time management.* Finally, when you know your life's purpose, you naturally manage time better. You don't want to procrastinate on things. Time flies when you're doing what you're meant to do. You don't waste time surfing the internet or watching dumb television shows. Your life becomes laser focused on things that serve your greater purpose.

Having an overarching sense of purpose is key to getting into the top 2% of your field. So how do you do it? How can you develop your sense of purpose if you haven't already? The Buddha said, "Your work is to discover your work and then with all your heart to give yourself to it."

FIND YOUR PURPOSE IN YOUR PAIN POINTS

The way to identify your overarching sense of purpose is to think about what things bother you the most.

For example, let's say you know a woman who is a health coach. She tells you that it drives her nuts when she goes to the grocery store and sees people who are clearly unhealthy filling their carts with junk food. She sees people with diseases that are caused by diet, and they're still filling their carts with junk food. It makes her so mad! It was this anger that led her to become a health coach and to start helping people see the connection between what they eat and the diseases they have.

She went back to school, learned about physiology and nutrition, and became a health coach because she was bothered by what she saw at the grocery store.

So, to find your purpose, think about what problems in life bother you the most. Perhaps it's animal rights or something to do with politics. Whatever it is, you can tell by the emotional charge you get by talking about it.

Does this mean you need to go and change your career? No, not at all. If you're passionate about animal rights, you don't need to become a veterinarian. Maybe you can write articles. Maybe you can volunteer at a shelter. Maybe you should become a vegetarian. You see, the overarching sense of purpose is what makes you REACH higher.

By finding your overarching sense of purpose and focusing on it, you'll find yourself with a drive and a passion you never felt before! As Dostoyevsky put it, "The secret of a man's being is not only to live, but to have something to live for." Find out what you're living for, and you'll be on your way to the STARS.

In the next chapter, we're going to start working our way around the STARS model and look at the first successful trait of the top 2%.

ENTREPRENEUR FOCUS
Four Steps to Finding Your Purpose

How do you find your purpose?

We live in a society where we're bombarded with stimuli. Now more than ever before, we're plugged into a rapidly evolving, wired world. The dings, rings, and buzzes that emanate from our smartphones seem to stop only when we forget to recharge.

But in those rare, quiet moments, we hear this internal voice telling us that life is supposed to be about more than just accumulating "stuff," achieving professional success and enjoying the moment. Life is supposed to have some deeper meaning or purpose.

But how do you find your purpose?

The quest to fill the void with a greater purpose is compelling. It sells books, seminars, and movies. It has been dramatized to such an extent that people are figuratively on the floor searching in the dark for the key that will unlock the secret to life contentment, purpose, and happiness.

But they never seem to find it. And you know why? Because they're looking in all the wrong places. Here are some tips for finding your focus.

Stop Looking for It

This may sound counterintuitive, but if you want to find your purpose, the first step is to stop looking for it. That's right. Get off your hands and knees. Stop thinking—and overthinking—about why you are here.

You'll never really know. We may get some clues about our place in the world, but full-on knowledge of why we are here might just be reserved for the afterlife. More important, trying to find your purpose has an inherent risk—you're assuming it's all about you.

You ask yourself, "What is my purpose that will help me feel fulfilled on a deeper level?" But here is the problem with this line of thought: Meaning and purpose come when we focus on others—not on ourselves.

If you really want to achieve your potential and live a more meaningful life, stop searching for purpose and start living with purpose.

Ask Yourself: "What Am I Needed For?"

Instead of concerning yourself with what you need or what you want, ask yourself: "What am I needed for?"

If you really want to make a change in this world, reflect on what's motivating you. Do you want to be the hero? If the answer is yes, then you are destined for misery. You won't find meaning helping others if you're really just trying to feel good or further your own interests. It's not about what you need. The question is—what is needed from you?

The good news is that you don't need to search very far. Opportunities are right in front of you—start with your friends, family, and community. Within your grasp are people in need. Start asking what you can do for them.

But here is the nuance that often trips people up. I'm not suggesting that you ask what is needed. There could be a security issue, but you may not be a police officer. There may be a health risk, but you may not be a doctor. You can't solve a problem you are not qualified to fix.

Instead, ask what you are needed for. What unique contribution can you bring to those in need? Identify the talents and interests that will allow you to be helpful and make an impact.

Take Action Steps

Your purpose relates to your talents, but you can't think your way to living with purpose. You don't find your purpose by listening to an inspirational audio series or contemplating philosophy on a mountaintop retreat. You find it in action.

Just like exercise, you have to start somewhere. Find or create an opportunity to contribute, volunteer, open a business, or take on additional responsibilities. Doing things to uniquely contribute to those around you should be part of your routine.

Without a concrete and sustainable action plan, the inspiration you're feeling now will eventually fizzle, and you'll wind up feeling empty and unsatisfied again. You don't need to start big—but you do need to get started. Find a way you can give your time and your talent to others on an ongoing basis. Once a week? Fine. Once a month? That's a start.

Review Where You Stand

You won't know where you stand without regular self-reflection. Every night, review what you did and ask yourself: Was that the best use of my time? Can I do more? Did I do too much? Can I delegate this, or should I spend more time doing it myself? Now you are learning by doing. That's how you live with purpose.

In truth, you don't just have one purpose. You have many. As you evolve, so will your purpose. When you were 15, your purpose may have been related to school, friends, and parents. At 35, it could be attached to your spouse or child.

When you live your life asking what you are needed for, you adapt, change, and grow. Along the way, you are able to contribute yourself to others—the ultimate purpose. Over time, you will gain insight into your unique purposes and better understand the things that only you can contribute.

In the end, whether you can pinpoint your purpose or not, you will have spent the better portion of your life helping others and living with purpose—which is always more valuable than finding it.

2

FUEL YOUR SUCCESS WITH PASSION

In the rest of the chapters, we're going to make our way around the STARS model. The image is a traditional five-pointed star. In the last chapter, we talked about the element that's at the top of the star—the Sense of Purpose. Going around counterclockwise is the next set of qualities that are common among those in the top 2% of their fields. These are what we're calling Traits.

Traits are the letter T in our STARS model and are the "personality traits" that the STARS have in common. Now, don't be misled by the term *personality traits*. These aren't things you're born with and if you don't have them, too bad. No, these are personality traits that can be LEARNED.

Personality traits can be learned. Researchers have studied the difference between temperament and personality traits. Temperament is something you're born with. Some babies are naturally more peaceful or calm and others are fussier and more easily excited. That's temperament. But what researchers have found is that personality is determined by an interaction between your temperament and your environment. Your parents, your schooling, the life experiences that you have all influence your personality. Your personality is shaped by the context that your temperament is in. Or, as noted American educator Virginia Voeks put it, "We learn only what we do. And what we do, we become. Live, therefore, in the ways you desire to have as part of your personality. Practice being the person you wish to become."

The four personality traits that the STARS have in common are something that you can absolutely learn to develop, too. Let's dig into the first trait in this chapter.

WHAT IS PASSION?

The first trait we're going to talk about is the trait of Passion. What exactly IS passion? We all use the word. "She feels very passionate about the subject." "They were in the heat of passion." But what does the word *passion* actually mean?

According to the dictionary, passion can have several meanings. It can have a religious meaning within Christianity. It can be a strong emotion or feeling, like "His ruling passion is greed." Or it can mean something that is a strong interest or an object of deep desire, such as "She developed a passion for the ballet."

For our purposes, we're going to combine two of those definitions. Passion, as we're defining it, is an intense, driving feeling or conviction toward an activity, object, or concept. In other words, passion is a *strong feeling* that is *directed toward something specific.*

Let's take a little side street in our conversation for a moment. As you can imagine, as executives at Nightingale-Conant, we've met many of the superstars in the personal development field. It's been an honor and a pleasure to have interacted with so many incredible thought leaders.

Here is what it's like to be in a room with some of these folks. We hear them on audio programs, or we see them on stage and we think, "Wow. That person is really passionate about what they're talking about." And they are. But you know what makes these people STARS? Not only are THEY passionate about what they're talking about, but they make YOU feel passionate about YOURSELF, too.

Here's an example. Anthony Robbins is one of our longtime authors. Here's a guy who is 6 feet 7 inches tall and has a booming voice. He's got a smile that literally radiates across the room. If you've seen him on stage or video, you know that he has an explosive energy that can captivate an audience. Well, let me tell you, he's the same way in person. What Tony does that makes him so successful is that he has a way of making people *feel passionate about themselves.* While he's always got brilliant ideas, what makes Tony TONY is that he can deliver those ideas with more passion than just about anybody I've ever met. It's not about presentation skills; it's about passion as we're defining it. Tony Robbins has a STRONG FEELING (to say the least) that is directed specifically at YOU.

Oprah Winfrey, as we mentioned earlier, has the same trait. She's got a passionate feeling that is directed at her audience. Everything she does, every show she has, every article she writes is done with the single intent of answering the question, "How will this benefit the audience?"

Now this isn't to say that passion is everything. It's not. Being passionate about something isn't a golden ticket to the STARS.

Passion is the *fuel* that drives you to the STARS. As Nightingale-Conant author Larry Winget puts it, "Excellence is what moves you to the top. And hard work doing the right things is what makes you excellent. To tell people that passion is the key to success does those folks a great disservice. Because somewhere down the road, they will discover that no one cares or shares their passion. They will find out that while they are passionate, they haven't *done the work* to be really good; they know nothing about selling or marketing, leadership, management, finance, their competition, serving customers, or all the other facets of a successful life or business. All they have is their passion. Try cashing that at the bank."

You see, this quote gets to the heart of the message of this chapter. Passion is the FUEL that will drive you to become excellent. If you have a passionate feeling, it's not enough. You have to translate that passionate feeling into directed, focused action. But taking actions without the fuel of passion doesn't work, either.

It's like when you were in school. You loved some classes and couldn't wait to get to class. But if you just sat there in the class, feeling passionate about the subject, but you didn't do your assignments and you didn't do them in an excellent manner, you wouldn't get a good grade in the class.

Similarly, there were probably other classes that dragged on and you couldn't wait for the class to be over. You had NO passion for the subject matter at all. You may have done the assignments and gotten a decent grade, but your performance was surely not as excellent as it would have been had you felt passionate about the subject.

The STARS who are in the top 2% of their fields are there because they FEEL passion and that passion has fueled them to become excellent.

So how can you develop a passion for something? How can you develop high-octane performance fuel for ANY AREA you want? The next three sections show you how.

Step 1: Fill Up the Tank

Think of something that you have little interest in. It might be video games or the mating habits of the African fruit fly. Do you have something in your mind right now? Stop and think about everything you know about that subject. Think about everything you know about the subject that you have little interest in. Chances are you don't actually KNOW much about the thing you have no passion for. But if you learned something interesting about it, you'd likely feel more passionate.

Have you ever had the experience of going to a museum exhibit or stumbling upon a documentary on a subject that you didn't know anything about previously? And you found yourself mesmerized thinking, "Wow! I didn't know that!" That's the dynamic I'm talking about. The more you know about something, the more you're going to find it interesting.

So, to increase your level of passion about something, fill up your tank! Learn as much as you can. Of course, it's going to be easier if it's a topic you're naturally interested in. But you can develop a passion for anything if you learn enough about it.

Step 2: Use High-Quality Fuel

We live in an information age. No matter what topic you're thinking about, there are hundreds of sources out there with information. Make sure you are using high-quality sources for your information. Be discerning. There is a huge difference between reading a tabloid newspaper and a textbook. Fill your tank up with high-quality fuel from sources that are trustworthy. If you're learning about time management, for example, Paris Hilton might not be the best source. Not that there's anything wrong with Paris Hilton, but she's not the first name that comes to mind when you think of time management. Look to people who are in the top 2% of the field you're studying and learn from them. Those are going to be the best sources of information.

Step 3: Drive All over Town

Have you ever been sitting in a room and someone bursts in the room and before they even say a word, they're conveying passion? You feel an energetic presence and will automatically give that person 100 percent of your attention. That's the third step. Once you've filled up your tank with high-quality fuel, take it all over town! Get excited about sharing your ideas with other people. It's not about being pushy, but it's about having so much passion and excitement about your subject that you WANT to tell people about it. Perhaps you have a friend who started an online radio show. He was so excited about this show that he had a T-shirt printed up and some business cards with the day and time of the show. Everywhere this man goes, he wears the shirt and hands out his cards. He's at the dry cleaner, the deli, the gas station saying, "Listen to my new show."

Or think about the stay-at-home dad who became so passionate about it that he started a national at-home dad's network.

Here's another story of someone who metaphorically drove all over town with her idea and ended up on TV! Kiersten Hathcock was a TV network marketing executive who quit her job to spend more time with her kids. She realized that all the kids' toy boxes she was seeing didn't fit into a modern décor, so she taught herself how to use power tools and invented one. She built a few pieces and took them to small outdoor markets. She developed a website and started contacting kids furniture stores in her town. She started using social media, which is the modern version of running all over town. She even appeared on *Shark Tank*, a national TV show that pairs venture capital investors with entrepreneurs. Talk about running all over town—this woman ran all over the world!

Think about how you can run all over town with your idea. Can you get some business cards printed? Can you go to shows? Join a club? Build a network? How can you get other people passionate about your passion?

Remember, we said earlier that one of the reasons that STARS are STARS is because not only do they have passion themselves, but they make YOU feel passionate, too. It's not enough to have your own passion. Spread that passion around! That's what makes the difference between a regular person and one of the STARS.

In our next chapter, we're going to talk about another trait of the STARS, an Innovative/Entrepreneurial Spirit.

ENTREPRENEUR FOCUS
Get Real and Find Your Passion

Every entrepreneur and hopeful business founder has likely heard the advice to do something he or she loves or can feel passionate about.

This advice has merit, as passion about an idea or product can really help drive a person to succeed. And if you don't believe in an idea or care about its success, it's harder to rise above the inevitable challenges, and this will show in the results.

But it might not always be easy to find a fun or exciting niche that's practical for business purposes. Whether you're looking to start an enterprise or earn a living or just want to feel more passionate about a current endeavor, looking within, setting goals, and shifting your perspective are helpful habits to practice.

Find a Niche

Working at something fun and interesting is what many people aspire to do. But identifying a special niche interest is a struggle for some people. Rather than focusing on turning a hobby into a business, be creative. Consider how your unique skills, quirks, or interests might translate into or transform a business.

For example, with a passion for the environment, someone could start a green consulting or marketing service. A love of exercise could be applied to personal training, fitness-related retail, or corporate health consulting.

Brainstorm about ways to improve or change a service, add a unique point of value to an existing sector, or meet an unmet need and thereby prompt your creativity to flow. Having something to excel at or a unique focus can be a powerful motivator.

Set Goals and Rewards

No matter what type of work someone does, his or her motivation can be enhanced by creating a target to shoot toward. Without setting goals, a person is simply floating around aimlessly. Pairing goals with rewards can be even more powerful.

The ability to set both short- and long-term goals is an important skill for anyone striving to succeed. Reaching a certain target brings a sense of accomplishment, fuels passion, stirs positive emotion, and encourages the flow of new ideas and energy.

Short-term goals should be specific and focused on what an individual wants to accomplish today or this week. They could involve making progress on a project, attaining a specific sales figure, or doing customer outreach. Longer-term goals should be fixed on the big picture over the months and years ahead. They might include a plan for growth, developing a product, or reaching another benchmark.

Setting sales, customer service, and productivity goals is often helpful for inspiring a passion to work through day-to-day tasks.

Knowing what to strive for and having a reward in sight can make work feel all the more exciting. Every task does not necessarily need a reward.

Try making the achievements fun. Keep short-term goals realistic, and ensure accountability if that helps inspire motivation. Make it a game. For example, try to "level up" by achieving a goal that unlocks a specific reward. Short-term goals could be tied to a favorite dinner or activity, while bigger achievements might be recognized with a vacation or a new gadget. Use whatever rewards drive the most motivation and gratification.

Change Your Perspective

Arriving at the right perspective and attitude is perhaps the most important factor in sustaining passion and enjoying an activity. Maintaining a negative view or a pessimistic outlook or remaining stuck in a rut puts a damper on motivation. These patterns can even turn a great business idea sour or simply create a toxic work environment.

Think about what you excel at—not what you lack, especially when first launching a new business. Focus on your end goals, not all the little steps you must take to get there.

When feeling worn down or burned out, step outside the normal routine and set aside some time for yourself outside work. Try to see your problems from someone else's point of view if an answer is not apparent. Or slip on those rose-colored glasses when things seem tough.

Enjoy What You Do

Achieving goals, seeing the excitement of growth, and looking at an old industry from a new perspective can help inspire a person's entrepreneurial spirit. And this makes it easier to work through the struggles of launching a company from the ground up.

As an entrepreneur, focusing on finding a unique benefit, setting goals, and being conscious of your unique perspective can prove helpful.

Each milestone reached can continue to offer entrepreneurial inspiration and make it easy to feel passionate about each day of work.

THE O.W.L. METHOD

n this chapter, we're talking about the second trait that is common among the STARS: an innovative or an entrepreneurial spirit. We're not necessarily talking about leaving your job or starting your own company. Sure, that's one way to express your entrepreneurial or innovative spirit. But it might just mean thinking a little differently about what you do every day. Mathematician James Yorke said it this way, "The most successful people are those who are good at Plan B."

In his essay, "Entrepreneur: What's in a Definition?" Peter Hupalo looks at how some small-business experts define the word "entrepreneur":

Bob Reiss, successful entrepreneur and author of *Low-Risk, High-Reward: Starting and Growing Your Small Business with Minimal Risk*, says: "Entrepreneurship is the recognition and pursuit of opportunity without regard to the resources you currently control, with confidence that you can succeed, with the flexibility to change course as necessary, and with the will to rebound from setbacks." A key factor in Reiss's definition is that entrepreneurs undertake opportunities *regardless of the resources the entrepreneur currently controls*.

Everyone has their own definition of entrepreneurship, but having an innovative spirit is a common hallmark. We'll explore that spirit in this chapter, starting with a quick quiz.

ARE YOU AN INNOVATOR?

Here is a short quiz to get you thinking about whether you've got an innovative or entrepreneurial spirit. There are only three questions, but your answers will tell you a lot about yourself.

Question 1: Are You a Born Entrepreneur?

Look back at your life. Did you have a lemonade stand? How about a car washing or lawn mowing business? Have you been trying to start one business or another since you were a kid?

If so, you're in good company. As a preteen, Steven Spielberg charged admission to his home movies (which involved wrecks he staged with his Lionel train set) while his sister sold popcorn. At the age of 12, his first production was complete, including a script and actors. Just one year later, at the age of 13, Spielberg won a prize for a 40-minute war movie he titled *Escape to Nowhere*. In 1963, at the young age of 16, his 140-minute production of *Firelight* (which would later inspire *Close Encounters*) was shown in a local movie theater and brought in a $100 profit.

Question 2: What Is Your WHY?

Nightingale-Conant author John Cummuta asks: What are the reasons you want to be an entrepreneur?

- Is it to get rich?
- Is it to get rid of a jerky boss?

- Is it to gain control over your life?
- Is it to pursue a dream vocation?

Some of these reasons are good, and some are not so good. For example, getting rid of a jerky boss is not a good one, because you will simply be exchanging one jerky boss for many potentially jerky bosses, called customers.

Getting rich, in and of itself, is also not a solid enough reason, because "rich" is hard to define, and "rich" is not really a destination in life. It's more like a stop along the way to a destination. Focusing on the destinations that are important to you would be more motivating.

How about having control over your daily life? Well, it's been said that the dictionary is the only place where "success" comes before "work." The entrepreneurial lifestyle allows freedom to set your own schedule, but this doesn't mean you can be lazy or casual about how you use your time. As business and success coach Brian Tracy says, you work 40 hours a week for survival. It's what you put in beyond 40 hours that contributes to your success.

Question 3: Are You Willing to Put in the Work?

You've also likely heard the cliché that we should work "smarter, not harder." Well, in the real world of the entrepreneur, you have to work smarter AND harder in the beginning. When John Cummuta first started the business that grew into tens of millions in annual revenue and landed him on *Inc.* magazine's *Inc. 500* list three times, he had a day job . . . and he kept it.

He described it this way: "I worked my job all day, then came home and worked on the business till it was nearly bedtime . . . sometimes long beyond bedtime. I was working as smart as I could . . . . and a lot harder than most folks are willing to."

Now, if you really answered these questions and have discovered that you are an entrepreneur, great! It can be one of the most money-multiplying strategies out there.

But what if, when you answered the questions in the quiz, you found that you aren't naturally an entrepreneur? Are you simply out of luck?

No! We've developed a method by which you can LEARN to have an entrepreneurial or innovative spirit. It's called the O.W.L. Method.

THE O.W.L. METHOD

In order to reach the top 2%, you have to use the O.W.L. method. It stands for *Own Win Leverage*.

You must have an attitude of OWNership over your work, you must have a WINning attitude of perseverance, and you must LEVERAGE what you've got into something more.

What does this mean?

Own

You have to OWN your work. It doesn't matter if you're the CEO of a company, if you have a small business you're running out of your garage, or if you work at a retail establishment, it's about having a sense of pride and ownership in what you do. Peter Drucker made an astute observation when he said, "The purpose of a business is to create a customer." And those who are in the top 2% understand that.

It's really interesting, but some of the most famous people in the world weren't seeking wealth or fame directly. The essence of the OWN part of the O.W.L. method is to develop the desire to be the BEST at whatever you're doing.

The second element of the O.W.L. method of entrepreneurship and innovation is *win*.

Win

I want to tell you a story that illustrates the principle of *win* in the Own/Win/Leverage method. Going along with our founding fathers theme, this has to do with George Washington, and the story comes from Adam Khan.

On his first military campaign, George Washington made a terrible mistake. The American colonies had not yet rebelled—that was 20 years down the road. Washington was working for Britain, which was in a cold war with France. The two countries were tussling with each other for territory all over the world, including the area near Virginia. One day Washington and his troops spotted a party of French camping in their territory and attacked them, killing ten men, and capturing the rest.

He shot first and asked questions later. He found out it was a diplomatic party, and one of the men he killed was an important French ambassador. Washington had made a big mistake. The two major military powers of that time ended their cold war and entered a hot war.

Imagine, for the moment, that you were Washington, and you made that mistake. What would you tell yourself about it? How would the mistake fit into the overall pattern of your life?

In other words: What kind of story do you live in? Where do you think you come from, and where do you think you're going?

You live by a story. Have you ever thought of it that way? Each of us has a story, and we are the main character in it. It's your life story, and it is the meaning of your life.

For example, one story Washington could have told himself was: "I am destined for failure." Compared to his contemporaries, he was poor. Killing the French ambassador could have been a final straw. He might have concluded that he wasn't cut out for military work and given up, climbed inside a bottle, and we might never have heard of him.

That's one story. That's one context within which he could have lived his life. Do you see that the story leads to certain feelings and actions consistent with the story?

Here's another possibility: He could have thought he was destined to make his mark in the world, and that his mistake was the most important lesson he was ever to learn. "Divine providence," he could have told himself, "is preparing me for a great task. I must learn all I can from this mistake for it may affect the future of the world."

Do you think he would feel differently about the circumstances of his life with this story? Of course, he would. Same circumstances, different story. But the heroic story would make him learn important military lessons from his mistake, and it would help him persist and endure hardships that would collapse a weaker person. The story would give him strength.

Judging by the letters he wrote home, the story he lived by was a lot more like this second one than the first one. And because he lived by that more inspiring story, he persisted and he learned and he did make a difference.

And that's the attitude we are talking about. To WIN you have to be persistent. You have to know that you're going to make it into that top 2%, and if something happens that looks like a problem, rewrite it into a powerful story that supports your success.

The final element of the O.W.L. method is *leverage*.

Leverage

By leverage we mean taking what you've got and using it to make more. Peter Drucker described it this way: "The entrepreneur always searches for change, responds to it, and exploits it as an opportunity."

Traditionally, leverage is a financial term, and that is part of it. The STARS know how to leverage money into more money. But it's also about leveraging opportunity. It's about taking something good that happens, even if it's small, and making it into something bigger.

So, to recap the O.W.L. method for developing an entrepreneurial or innovative spirit, you must take OWNership of your work, you must have a WINning attitude regardless of what happens to you, and you must LEVERAGE the events of your life into something greater.

BE AN INNOVATEUR

Before we end this chapter, let's clarify something about entrepreneurship, innovation, and the O.W.L. method.

Do you have to work on your own to be an O.W.L.? No. There are three ways to use the O.W.L. method.

1. You can be a person working for a company who wishes to become an entrepreneur.
2. You can be an existing entrepreneur who already has a business.

3. Or you can be an intrapreneur (a person who works in an existing company, but in the capacity of an entrepreneur within the organization).

But we've come up with a term that describes all three of these types of O.W.L.s. If you want to be in the top 2% of your company, field, or industry, you have to become an *INNOVATEUR*. An Innovateur is someone, whether they are in a job, leading a company, an independent worker, or don't even work outside the home, but they have an innovative attitude. They OWN their success. They have a WINning attitude. And they know how to LEVERAGE small things and make them bigger.

Let's explore the qualities of an Innovateur:

1. *They don't follow the crowd.* We've given lots of examples in this program of people who did something different. Whether it's teaching yourself how to use power tools so that you can make your own toy boxes or starting a new country, Innovateurs don't follow the crowd.
2. *They take action when innovation happens.* If you get a great idea while you're driving, pull over and call your own voicemail with a reminder about the idea. If you get an inspiration while you're doing the dishes, stop and act on it! The dishes can wait.
3. *They listen to their intuition.* Innovateurs get a "gut feeling" about something. They listen to that inner voice, and it's what guides their decisions.

To truly innovate, you have to be willing to overcome your fears and often go with your gut instincts. Harnessing the power of "right place, right time" doesn't hurt, either. Innovateurs not only know when to act on a business opportunity, but they know how to mitigate their risk and take the leap when it's worth it.

We have covered a lot of ground in this chapter! In the next one, we'll talk about the third trait of the STARS, a strong self-image.

ENTREPRENEUR FOCUS
How to Recognize Opportunities for Innovation

Every business will reach inflection points where change is inevitable. Failure to change at these points may cause your business to lose momentum and die. Although there is no "wrong" time to innovate, there are several critical points in the growth of your organization that demand innovative thinking.

Any viable business plan includes a system for regularly identifying, developing, and protecting innovative ideas. But there are times where your business needs an extra boost of innovation to break through an inflection point. Recognizing these inflection points and responding with innovation will accelerate business growth to a new level.

Expanding into a New Market

When your business moves into a new market, it is up against other companies with an established customer base. To gain traction in the new market, you need to stand out from the competition. Study the market and existing products to pinpoint problems with those products or to identify unmet needs in the market. Use these problems or unmet needs as opportunities to innovate and develop products (or product features) that deliver a competitive edge. If you can burst into the new market with a fresh product and "must have" features, you can quickly establish your position as a market leader.

New Product Launch

New products give your company a chance to increase revenue and reach more customers. When developing a new product, don't just bring in your existing development team. Involve people throughout the organization in the innovation process, such as employees in the sales, marketing, and customer service departments. Including these members of your team provides a broader view of the industry and customer needs, which can generate more innovative and applicable ideas. Use the new product launch as an opportunity to further distinguish your company and its products from competitors in the market. In my work as an innovation strategist, I have seen many cases where a single new product is responsible for the exponential growth of the company. So don't just create another "me too" product; launch something that will generate a powerful buzz in the industry.

Changes in Your Industry

Changes in your industry and overall market trends require you to adapt your products to meet these changes and adjust your strategy to leverage the new market trends. Some changes occur quickly while others develop over time. For rapid industry changes, you need to swiftly develop creative ideas to modify existing products based on the changes. For slower changes, such as evolving market trends, focus your innovation activities on the new problems that will be created by the market trends. Identify innovative solutions to these problems so your company can be prepared with ready solutions to the problems when they arise. These solutions put you a step ahead of the competition because you anticipated the problems and solved them in advance.

New Competitors

A new kid on the block is the perfect catalyst to innovate features that can set your product apart from the competition. If your business has been operating for a while, you already have an existing customer base. Leverage that advantage by obtaining feedback from your current customers to identify ways to improve your products. Examine problems routinely handled by your customer service department— these problems represent opportunities to innovate. Use your existing position in the market to your advantage and find ways to distinguish your product offerings from the new competitors. It's important to act quickly to engage your innovation team and identify ways to preserve (and hopefully expand) your market share.

Seeking Investment Capital

Many organizations seek to raise capital at various points during the growth of the company. Savvy investors evaluate a company's competitive position in their market and the protection of proprietary systems and procedures. But just as important to an investor is your proven ability to innovate. If your company is anticipating a need for a capital investment, consider boosting your innovation efforts to identify creative ideas that can make your products stand out from the competition. And when you identify innovations that provide a strong competitive edge, secure an appropriate form of intellectual property protection to maintain your exclusive use of those innovations. These additional intellectual property assets can improve company valuation and the attractiveness of your company to investors.

If your business is approaching any of these inflection points, start planning your innovation activities today so you can successfully navigate through the critical transitions. By developing an innovation action plan now, you can regularly produce innovative ideas and have an arsenal of valuable ideas at hand when you reach one of these points.

SHEDDING YOUR SELF IMPOSTER

In this chapter we're going to talk about self-image. To illustrate the power of self-image and the theme of this chapter, we're starting with a Japanese parable.

Long ago in a small, far away village, there was place known as the House of 1,000 Mirrors. A small, happy little dog learned of this place and decided to visit. When he arrived, he bounced happily up the stairs to the doorway of the house. He looked through the doorway with his ears lifted high and his tail wagging as fast as it could. To his great surprise, he found himself staring at 1,000 other happy little dogs with their tails wagging just as fast as his. He smiled a great smile and was answered with 1,000 great smiles just as warm and friendly. As he left the house, he thought to himself, "This is a wonderful place. I will come back and visit it often."

In this same village, another little dog, who was not quite as happy as the first one, decided to visit the house. He slowly climbed the stairs and hung his head low as he looked into the door. When he saw the 1,000 unfriendly looking dogs staring back at him, he growled at them and was horrified to see 1,000 little dogs growling back at him. As he left, he thought to himself, "That is a horrible place, and I will never go back there again."

You see, that is the power of self-image. All the faces in the world are mirrors. If the people in your life are selfish, unhappy, unhealthy, angry, or negative, that is nothing more than a mirror for what is going on inside of you. Alternatively, if the people who surround you inspire you, and show you love, resilience, integrity, happiness, and positivity, then you clearly have a strong self-image.

The STARS understand that for others to see us as valuable, we first have to value ourselves. Norman Vincent Peale said, "People become really quite remarkable when they start thinking that they can do things. When they believe in themselves, they have the first secret of success."

SELF-IMAGE, SELF-ESTEEM, AND SELF-REGARD

Before we go any further, let's make an important clarification. What is the difference between self-image, self-esteem, and self-regard? You often hear the terms used interchangeably, but are they really the same thing. Does it mean the same thing to say, "She has a strong self-image" "She has high self-esteem," and "She has high self-regard?"

While they sound similar, there are some important distinctions. Self-esteem can be described as feeling good about yourself. If you have high self-esteem, you feel good about yourself, and if you have low self-esteem, you don't feel good about yourself. This is a changeable thing, from moment to moment. Surely you've experienced it. You're going along one day, feeling good about yourself and then someone says something critical. Your boss says something negative, or your mother criticizes you. Suddenly, you go from feeling great about yourself to feeling low. You see, self-esteem is something that changes from day to day, moment to moment.

And here's something you may not know. Remember all those programs that were designed to boost self-esteem? Well, research shows that there really isn't a strong correlation between self-esteem and success. In fact, one study found that many convicted criminals (especially drug kingpins) had high self-esteem. Another study calls it "compensatory self-inflation," meaning that people often tend to overinflate their self-esteem to compensate for the threat of failure—especially if the failure is public rather than private. So, self-esteem is not really a stable enough construct for us to be using it here.

What about self-image? According to Dr. Joe Rabino, "A person's self-image is the mental picture, generally of a kind that is quite resistant to change, that depicts not only details that are potentially available to objective investigation by others (height, weight, hair color, sex, I.Q. score, is this person double-jointed, etc.), but also items that have been learned by that person about himself or herself, either from personal experiences or by internalizing the judgments of others. Those items include the answers to such questions as:

- Am I skinny?
- Am I fat?
- Am I attractive?
- Am I weak?
- Am I strong?
- Am I intelligent?
- Am I stupid?
- Am I a good person?
- Am I a bad person?
- Am I masculine?
- Am I feminine?
- Am I likable?

A simple definition of a person's self-image is their answer to this question: "What do you believe people think about you?" A more technical term for self-image that is commonly used by social and cognitive psychologists is self-schema. Like any schema, self-schemas store information and influence the way we think and remember. So, really, self-image is a more stable construct because it develops over time.

What, then, is self-regard? Well, basically, for our purposes, self-regard is how much you like your self-image. Self-regard suggests having more respect for oneself, which might involve temporarily having lower self-esteem. One example of this might be if you fail a test. You might lower your self-esteem temporarily—you do not "feel good" about yourself for not giving your best on the test, and because of your high self-regard, you vow to study harder and give your best on your next test.

YOUR MENTAL BLUEPRINT FOR SUCCESS

How is it that the self-image is so powerful in determining whether or not you reach the STARS? Nightingale-Conant author Maxwell Maltz describes it best in his program *Psycho-Cybernetics*. He says, "Whether we realize it or not, each of us carries about with us a mental blueprint or image of ourselves. It may be vague or ill-defined to our conscious gaze. But it is there, complete down to the last detail. This self-image is our own conception of "the sort of person I am." It has been built up from our beliefs about ourselves. But most of these beliefs about ourselves have unconsciously been formed from our past experiences, our successes and failures, our humiliations, our triumphs, and the way other people have reacted to us, especially in early childhood. From all these, we mentally construct a "self" or a picture of a self. Once an idea or belief about our self goes into this picture, it becomes "true" as far as we are personally concerned. We do not question its validity but proceed to act upon it just as if it were true.

This self-image becomes a golden key to living a better life because of two important discoveries. One, all of your actions, feelings, behaviors, even your abilities, are ALWAYS consistent with this self-image. You will act like the sort of person you believe yourself to be. Not only this, but you literally cannot act otherwise, in spite of all your conscious efforts or willpower. The person who believes that he or she is a victim of injustice, for example, will find him or herself attracting people and circumstances that confirm that belief. And two, self-image can be changed.

What's interesting about this is that Maltz was a plastic surgeon. He became interested in the psychology of self-esteem after he started noticing the dramatic and sudden changes in people's personalities when a perceived facial defect was corrected. He shares stories of the shy and retiring man who became bold and courageous. Or the "stupid" boy who changed into an excellent student. Perhaps the most startling of all is the hardened criminal who changed almost overnight into a model prisoner who got paroled and became a responsible member of society.

So, are we saying you should run out and book an appointment with a plastic surgeon? No. Not at all.

Some of Maltz's patients would complain—even after an impressive reconstruction procedure—that they couldn't see the difference and would state that they still felt ugly. Maltz realized that this was a product not of the image they were seeing in the mirror, but of the image that they had of themselves in their minds.

Was it their ears, nose, or some other physical feature that caused these personality and character changes? No. It was how these people FELT about themselves that made the difference.

Whatever you perceive your imperfection to be, there is another person with the same issue who doesn't see it as a problem. Do you have a big nose? Barbra Streisand does, too, and it hasn't held her back. Are you too short? Actor Danny DeVito is barely 5 feet tall. And at 5 feet 3 inches, Muggsy Bogues was the shortest basketball player to ever play in the NBA. Maybe you're too tall. As we've mentioned, Anthony Robbins is 6 feet seven inches. It hasn't really been a problem for him. Maybe you're overweight. So was George Foreman when he came back at the age of 40 to win an additional 31 fights, weighing in at around 267 pounds.

You see? Self-image isn't based on what's reality. It's based on your BELIEFS about yourself. In order to change your self-image, you have to change your beliefs about yourself.

We have clearly established the importance of a strong self-image to being in the top 2%. We've also learned that it's pretty deeply ingrained but that it CAN be changed. So, how can you go about changing your self-image? What are some things you can do to shed your self imposter and reveal the essence of who you really are?

SHEDDING YOUR SELF IMPOSTER

Here is a model that is useful as imagery to illustrate the proper balance. We call it the Self-Regard Continuum. On the left side, you see a very small person. This represents someone with low self-regard or someone who doesn't like his or her self-image. On the far right side of the continuum, you see a very large representation of a person. This is someone who is overly confident or has an overly inflated sense of him- or herself. We've all met people like that, right? And in the middle of the continuum is a medium-sized representation of a person. This is a person who has a healthy sense of self—one who values him- or herself, but also understands that he or she isn't perfect and is striving to improve at all times.

If you have too little self-regard, you'll underestimate yourself and keep yourself down by not taking advantage of opportunities and the good things in life. If you have too much self-regard, you won't be open to new learning or new experiences.

Here are some tips to help you achieve the perfect balance of self-regard. The self-image is changed not through intellectual knowledge, but through experience. As stated previously, that's how you developed your self-image in the first place: through the experiences you've had in the past.

Reframe Failure

If you have low self-regard, you probably haven't viewed a lot of your past experiences as successful. There are two ways you can rectify this. One is to go back and look at a perceived failure and reframe it. Most people who have bounced back from a serious illness or failure of some kind will tell you that right in the middle of the problem is an opportunity for something equally positive. The greater the tragedy, the greater the opportunity. Author and motivational speaker Leo Buscaglia said it this way: "We seem to gain wisdom more readily through our failures than through our successes. We always think of failure as the antithesis of success, but it isn't. Success often lies just on the other side of failure." Here's a short description of how visualizing and saying affirmations can improve your self-esteem.

When we think thoughts or say words, the neurons in our brains release certain chemicals. Over time, pathways are formed in the brain, kind of like roads or canyons. The more often we repeat a thought, behavior, or a statement, the stronger that pathway gets. If we repeat something enough, it becomes like the Grand Canyon in our brain. BUT we can change it by thinking or saying something different. Even if we don't necessarily BELIEVE what we are saying or thinking, the brain chemistry changes anyway. Pretty soon, with enough repetition, a NEW road or canyon starts to be built. And before you know it, that's the pathway that becomes automatic.

Obviously that is an oversimplified explanation of the field of neurology, but you get the idea. When Earl Nightingale said, "You become what you think about," he meant your brain becomes what you think about.

OK, let's try it here. Let's do an exercise called Virtual Reality Imaging. It's kind of like visualization for the modern age. Here is how you do Virtual Reality Imaging: Think of a time when you felt confident in yourself. Try and choose a period in your life, rather than a specific experience or event. Think of a time in your life when your self-image was strong.

Now, take a moment to relax. Breathe deeply and let your body sink into your chair. Close your eyes. Now think about that time in your life when you felt great, when your body was as healthy as it could be and your life was great.

Notice how you are dressed in your mental picture. What does your complexion look like? How is your energy level? Use all your senses to create a virtual image of yourself at that time in your life. Notice the smile on your face. Breathe.

As you breathe, draw in that image so it deeply penetrates your body. Feel the energy and confidence that you have in the image. Imagine that image stepping into yourself right now. Like a ghost, let the image of yourself step into your self-image now. Let that feeling of confidence and positive self-regard fill you up from within. Hold that picture for a few moments while I pause.

Now open your eyes. How do you feel? Remember, the more often you do the Virtual Reality Imaging technique, the more your brain will begin to form those patterns and the faster this self-image will become the permanent one.

Similarly, the next time you find yourself saying a negative statement, such as "I am terrible with directions. I couldn't find my way out of a paper bag." Stop and change what you're saying: "I'm pretty good at finding my way around."

CONTROL YOUR EGO

OK, but what if you have overly HIGH self-regard? Chances are you don't, or else you wouldn't be reading this book. People with overly high self-regard don't tend to invest in a lot of learning experiences. But here are some suggestions to help you stay well-balanced as you start to move into the top 2% of your field. It's easy to let your ego get the best of you.

To stay humble, learn something new. Martial arts is a great example. No matter who you are or what you've done elsewhere, if it's your first day of karate, you will be wearing a white belt. The white belt in karate symbolizes having an open mind.

Another tip is to stay focused on something bigger than yourself. Robert Schuller says, "Goals must never be from your ego, but problems that cry for a solution."

Also, surround yourself with people who are different from you. Diversity is a good thing at helping you stay balanced. Just because you value something doesn't mean it's the only thing of value. Don't be afraid to listen when someone tells you you're wrong. Or, as Oscar Wilde put it, "Whenever too many people agree with me, I feel I must be wrong."

So, how can you use this concept of self-image and self-regard to become one of the STARS? Are you still growing? Are you presenting yourself with opportunities that challenge yourself to grow? It's not always about "feeling good about yourself." No. In fact, in order to become one of the highest-paid, highest-profile people in your industry, you're going to have to grow. You're going to have to try new things, and you're going to fail. But as long as you keep getting back up again and reaching for new heights, you WILL find yourself among the STARS.

In our next chapter, we'll cover the final trait in our STARS model, enthusiasm.

ENTREPRENEUR FOCUS
How to Stop Undermining Your Self-Esteem

It is easy to lose track of your worth after you have spent significant time in an unhealthy work environment. If you were given too little, you may view yourself as lacking and believe you are inadequate. If you were starved for recognition, you may become hard on yourself and insecure in conflictual situations because you fear being seen as wrong and being fired.

Conversely, if you were given too much, you may have become dependent upon other people to fill you up and make you feel happy and successful, perhaps becoming angry or abusive when the world doesn't shift on its axis to give you what you want when you want it. When you have never been held responsible for sustaining your own success or well-being, you remain emotionally immature and demanding.

Change Your Inner Dialogue

To increase your self-esteem, improve the way you talk to yourself. Stop the inner dialogue that you are not good enough or that you must repeatedly prove your worth. That causes you to be inauthentic and to overfunction.

Conversely, if you only feel good enough when people are bending over backward to placate your needs, you will suffer from the disappointment of unmet and unrealistic expectations. That will cause you to become angry and demanding, and to feel empty.

Find Balance

If you are not getting your important needs met because you put yourself second to meeting the needs of others, start putting your needs first. When you put yourself first, you give yourself the sense of importance you so desperately seek from others.

If, on the other hand, you expect others to put you first and do everything for you, you will never develop the all-important empathy necessary for sustaining healthy connections. Find the balance of what you need to do for yourself and what you can realistically expect from others.

Know Your Worth

If your worth is dependent upon pleasing others, you will come up empty. Nothing you do for others will be enough to make you feel valued and appreciated in the way you desire. Knowing your worth has to come from within. Your worth is determined by the treatment you accept or expect for yourself, not by how much of yourself you give away.

Conversely, you cannot gain the skill of developing your own self-worth if you expect others to constantly soothe you, build you up, and make you feel like you are a success. Measuring your worth by how important others make you feel makes your sense of self too dependent on other people.

To know your worth, take charge of yourself and see how it feels to experience your own power.

Create Your Own Happiness

Neither success nor happiness are givens. They are creations. If happiness is not developed from within, you will naturally start looking for happiness from outside sources. This makes you needy. Your expectations, driven by insecurity, will drain others or push them away.

Trust that you deserve success and happiness. Figure out how to self-soothe and make yourself happy. When you enjoy your own achievements and success, your sense of worth will attract new opportunities and the recognition you deserve from your bosses and coworkers.

Be Proud

Do things you are proud of. Take care to dress nice. Be nice, be calm, be loving, and have boundaries. Work hard, achieve all you can, be clean and be kind. Kindness will take you further in life than any other human characteristic.

Walk tall. There is so much about you that is good, regardless of what you have been told. Choose to believe in who you are and be proud of that. Do not compare yourself to others. Like the snowflake, you are not repeatable.

Work Hard

Happiness is a by-product of achieving and having a purpose. Hard work trumps genius, so let go of the idea you must have a stellar IQ to be successful. The hard workers in life, void of entitlement, are the people who succeed at the highest levels.

There is nothing that can make you feel better about yourself than being committed in life, to your life, and to yourself through hard work. With hard work, success is a guarantee. Success naturally brings us self-love, self-respect, self-esteem, recognition, and happiness.

Exercise

Exercise is good all around. First, it is the best anti-anxiety and anti-depressive agent around. It promotes a positive mood, and it helps you feel good about your physique. Nothing can lower self-esteem more quickly than not liking what you look like.

Commit to exercising a minimum of three times per week, and do what you can to get outdoors. When you get outside, it yanks you out of the daily grind, and you are reminded of how beautiful this earth is, how beautiful life is, and how much you have to be thankful for.

Eat Healthy

What you feed your stomach, you feed your brain. The digestive system is the most similar in neurochemistry to the brain, which is why your stomach is considered your second brain. To feel good and be happy, eat healthy.

Supply your brain with the nutrients that stimulate health and positive mood. Eat lots of greens and drink a lot of water. Eat low-fat proteins to fuel your body for a positive mood, productivity, and sustainable energy.

Choose Healthy Connections

It only takes one toxic person to destroy your entire sense of self. Choose people, companies, or bosses that treat you with dignity and respect. Refuse to participate in relationships where you have to constantly prove your worth to keep their interest. Conversely, to have healthy a self-esteem, avoid being that person who demands that others constantly bend to your needs for you to feel alive and worthy.

Depend on Yourself

Do not allow others to do for you what you can do for yourself. There is no path to a healthy self-esteem through being lazy or entitled. Learn to take care of your own needs and be responsible for your own success. Support your life in all the ways you can.

Take control and become a whole person you can admire, depend upon, and trust.

Let Others Be Themselves

If you are needy, insecure, entitled, or demanding, you become controlling. When you are controlling, you compromise the freedoms of the important people in your life through fear, abandonment, or engulfment. When you love yourself, you will not need to make demands because you will already have your needs taken care of. This makes you easier to work with and for.

People will respond to you the most when you give them the freedom to be themselves.

Be Happy for Others

People with healthy self-esteem seldom feel jealousy or envy because they are satisfied in their own lives, careers, and relationships. They are satisfied with who they are as people. Be happy for other people and their happiness. This shift will fundamentally change your life and only serve to bring happiness your way.

Trust there is enough love, money, happiness, and success for everyone. When you see there is no such thing as lack, other people's success or happiness will no longer be a threat to you and your view of yourself. Your self-worth is YOUR business.

CHAPTER

5

THE ALWAYS ON™ PROCESS

In this chapter we're going to talk about the last trait of the highest-paid, highest-profile people in ANY industry—high energy and enthusiasm.

Kids have unbridled energy and passion. They hit the ground running first thing in the morning, go-go-go all day long, and literally have to be forced to go to sleep at night. Then, the next day, they do it again.

But, for most people, that eventually changes. They discover the snooze button on their alarms. Instead of jumping out of bed to greet the day, they roll over for ten more minutes of sleep. Instead of playing until their eyelids droop, most people plop in front of the TV, sitting there until they doze off. What happened? More important, does it happen to everyone?

Well, we have identified that the highest-paid, highest-profile people who are at the top 2% of any industry DON'T lose their enthusiasm and energy. Or, if they lose it, they get it back, and that's what gets them to the top.

Consider the world's top CEOs. Many of them start their day with energy and enthusiasm and make it last all day long. But notice that these folks kept stoking the fire of energy with things that give them life balance. They don't work ALL the time. No, they take time for their kids and family, they exercise, they engage in activities that RE-ENERGIZE them throughout the day. Or, as Nightingale-Conant author Dale Carnegie put it, "If you want to BE enthusiastic, ACT enthusiastic."

THE ALWAYS ON ™ PROCESS

How can YOU develop the ability to be high energy and have enthusiasm like those in the top 2%? We've developed a process that will help you to skyrocket your physical, mental, and spiritual energy. It's called The Always On™ Process. Here's how it works.

Every day, you need to replenish your energy in each of three areas: physical energy, mental energy, and spiritual energy. You can start by identifying what times of the day you need to focus on replenishing yourself in each of the areas.

For example, if you're a "morning person," you might feel most physically or mentally energetic at that time. You may want to engage in some spiritual practice first thing in the morning to boost that energy and set the stage for the rest of the day. Then, as the day moves on, your physical energy might wane. You'll want to engage in thoughts or behaviors that re-energize yourself physically. Similarly, many of us experience a dip in mental energy in the afternoon. For that, we've developed a unique process called The *Always On™ Process*. The Always On™ Process teaches you what to do to reclaim that mental energy so that you can stay focused. Now, some people might call themselves "night people," and for them, the process might be reversed.

Here are some things you can do in the morning. For physical energy, eat breakfast and exercise. We saw how valuable those activities were to the CEOs we learned about earlier. For mental energy, you might do a mental Photo Shopping exercise. This is where you create a mental image of yourself as an energetic, enthusiastic person, and then see that person stepping into the image of the current you, replacing your low-energy self with a high-energy version of you. And if you need a spiritual boost in the morning, go outside and have your morning coffee or tea in the garden or on your patio. Oprah Winfrey makes it a practice to go into a special prayer room in her house every single morning before she goes to work. It may only be two minutes, or it could be 20 minutes, depending on the day. But she starts each day connecting to her spirit.

What about in the afternoon? What are some energy boosters you can do in the middle of a busy day? Music is a great energizer! Listen to some uplifting motivational music. As German poet Berthold Auerbach says, "Music washes away from the soul the dust of everyday life." Have some fruit and protein, like an apple and a cheese stick, if you find your physical energy lagging. Or go for a little walk and drink some water. And if your mental energy is starting to dip, close your eyes and take a five-minute mental vacation. Just imagine yourself in your favorite vacation spot for five minutes.

Now, in the evening, how about trying something we like to call the Happiness Hour? Most of us know about Happy Hour, where people go to a bar and eat fattening food, drink expensive drinks, and shout at each other over the sounds of sports on TV. Instead, why not implement a Happiness Hour? A Happiness Hour is a period of time after you get home from work where you sit down and reconnect with the people you love. It might involve you, your spouse, and your children going out onto the patio or deck or into the living room with a glass of wine or sparking juice and sharing about your day. Or, if you live alone or no one else is available, do it yourself. Sit down, relax, and think about what went right today. Think about the positive things you accomplished and what you're grateful for this day. It doesn't have to be a whole hour. Like Oprah's prayer practice, even if it's just a few minutes to transition from your external work life into your personal private life, the Happiness Hour can be a great way to center yourself.

Use Mental Subtitles

OK, so we've gone through the different times of the day and talked about how to manage your energy during the various times you might find your energy lagging. But there's one more area that we need to cover, and it goes a bit deeper. What do you do when you're faced with certain people, places, situations, or circumstances that just suck the life right out of you? Most of us have things we need to do that we really don't want to do, and it's hard to be at the top of our game when we're doing it. How does the Always On™ Process work then?

Here is a technique you can use that can help you stay positive and enthusiastic, regardless of what you're doing. It's called Mental Subtitles. Here's how it works. Let's say you've got to do something you don't want to do. Maybe it's having dinner with your mother-in-law. As you arrive at her house, mentally imagine that you're watching a movie that has subtitles. You know how when you see foreign films and they have subtitles that run across the bottom that tell you what is going on? That's what this is. So you walk up to the door and your mother-in-law embraces your spouse. The subtitle might say, "She misses her child." If she gives you a snide look or makes an obnoxious comment, the subtitle says, "She feels threatened that you took her baby away."

See how this works? By using Mental Subtitles, you can step out of the moment and rise to a higher level of energy. Let's do another one. You have to go to a committee meeting at work, and you hate them. These are really low energy times for you, and you find yourself dozing off during these meetings. Instead, as you're walking into the meeting, turn on your Mental Subtitles. That annoying lady from accounting? She's worried about getting laid off. The sales manager who is giving that PowerPoint presentation? He's nervous that everyone will think his presentation is boring. Use the Mental Subtitles technique to help you move into a more compassionate place about the people and events of your life. This will raise your energy in these situations.

Always On™ in Action

Finally, let's see how the Always On™ Process looks in action. Glen is a marketing director for a large hotel chain. In 1989 he married the love of his life, Gina. They took a honeymoon cruise to the Caribbean and shortly after they got back, they found out that Gina was pregnant. Unfortunately, they also found out that they both had contracted the HIV virus. At the time, HIV was an death sentence. They were fortunate that their daughter Olivia was born HIV negative, but they both had to live with the reality that they might not see her grow up.

Glen, however, epitomizes the Always On™ Process for energy management. Every morning, Glen exercises. He eats a nutritious breakfast. He writes down his goals for the day and then goes off to work. While at work, he manages his physical energy. Because his immune system is compromised, he makes sure to eat a lot of fresh fruits and vegetables. He takes a lot of medications, but instead of cursing the fact that he has to take 35 pills a day, he says a silent prayer of gratitude that he has the medication that keeps him alive. He knows that there are millions of others with HIV who don't have the same access to medication as he does. Every night as he climbs into bed he thinks about how grateful he is that he got to spend another day with his wife and daughter. Glen greets each day with enthusiasm and energy. He doesn't feel physically great 100 percent of the time, but on those days where his physical energy is lacking, he focuses on the spiritual and mental. He firmly believes that the reason he is alive today is because he manages his physical, mental, and spiritual energy. In this way, Glen is definitely one of the STARS.

By consciously managing your energy in terms of physical energy, mental energy, and spiritual energy, you'll be able to make the most of each day. You'll be energized and enthusiastic about your life, which is a key trait of those who are in the top 2%.

In our next chapter, we'll move on to the next arm of the star in our STARS model: Attitude.

ENTREPRENEUR FOCUS
How to Boost Your Entrepreneurial Energy

The road to success is paved with full days, heavy workloads, and a 24/7 schedule. An entrepreneur's life can be exhausting, yet your overall success hinges on your ability to push through and keep at it, day in and day out.

Maintaining your energy over the long haul is key, but everyone gets run down. Whether you're feeling in a slump or just need a pick-me-up, here are 14 effective ways you can rev up your engines and keep hitting your stride.

Control Your Stress

Stress can create overwhelming feelings of anxiety, worry, and tension, all of which take up huge amounts of energy and leave you feeling zapped and uninspired. It's important that you find healthy ways to deal with stress and to recognize what may be setting you off, so you can find ways to manage your stress.

Try keeping a stress diary where you can record information about what is stressing you out and why. You can use a template to make it easier to make regular entries, throughout your day or week, so you can see if there are patterns when you feel particularly overwhelmed and then find ways to better handle it.

Take a Cold Shower

Taking a warm, steamy shower is so relaxing, but first thing in the morning it can leave you feeling drowsy—not a good way to start a high-energy day. To help you get your day going, try turning the knob toward cold—or as lukewarm as you can stand—for the last 30 seconds.

Doing so can help improve circulation and stimulate your nervous system, which produces an antidepressant effect. A few seconds of discomfort, and you'll emerge feeling refreshed and energized.

Take a Coffee Break

Coffee is a natural stimulant and can help increase wakefulness, alleviate fatigue, and improve focus. But according to researchers, you can ensure you get the most out of your latte by timing your coffee intake around the natural rise and fall of your cortisol levels.

If you drink coffee first thing in the morning, you may end up with a "wired up" jittery feeling. Cortisol levels dip several hours after you wake up, which is a good window for a caffeine boost. For most people, the best time to drink a caffeinated drink is a between 9:30 A.M. and 11:30 A.M. Avoid drinking caffeine in the afternoon as this can lead to insomnia.

Eat a Light Lunch

You skipped breakfast or munched on a doughnut, and now it's lunchtime and you're starving. That mega-burger is calling your name, but if you're hoping to avoid that post-lunch slump, you'll pick something lighter.

Eating a big meal puts your digestive process into overdrive, using up a lot of your body's energy and leaving you wanting to take a nap at your desk. Try eating a light lunch and focus on foods with whole grains, lean protein, and healthy fats. Skip eating anything sugary or high in carbohydrates, like bread, pasta, rice, or potatoes, as these can boost the production of serotonin, which can make you feel groggy.

Drink Plenty of Water

Our bodies are made up of about 60 percent water. When you don't get enough of it, you end up dehydrated, which can leave you feeling fatigued and drained. Meanwhile, drinking enough water will help speed up your metabolism, rid your body of toxins, help speed digestion, circulate blood, and keep your mouth from drying out. Water is also important for brain function and will help you feel more awake and alert.

Keep Your Body Fueled

Make sure you're giving your body what it needs to perform optimally. Try eating healthy snacks, with a steady supply of nutrients and energy, every few hours. Oftentimes, if you're feeling stressed, it's tempting to grab a high-carb or high-sugar snack.

But it's best to avoid foods high in sugar, which can cause a spike your insulin levels, only to leave you feeling hungry and sleepy in a few hours. And before you start munching away, make sure you're actually hungry, and not simply giving into food cravings or filling down time.

Get Physical

Exercise increases your endorphin levels, which are the hormones that are released when we do something that requires a burst of energy. If you're feeling lethargic and blah, get moving!

Exercise will perk you up immediately and help you increase your focus and attention, not to mention improve your overall health by lowering cholesterol and blood pressure and improving your sleep. Consistently working out has also been shown to reduce levels of depression and boost your mood.

Practice Yoga and Meditation

If feelings of stress and anxiety are leaving you feeling drained and overwhelmed, yoga and meditation may be just the thing you need. Both of these practices can be part of a routine of self-care that leaves you feeling relaxed and empowered to take on new challenges.

According to one study, doing 25 minutes of yoga can boost brain function and energy. Practicing yoga and doing daily meditations can promote a mental state of calm and peace, and help you focus your attention.

Get Some Sun

Our modern lifestyle keeps us indoors and under artificial lights, and it may be messing with body systems and making us function less than optimally. Not getting enough exposure to natural daylight may have an effect on your mood, making you feel lethargic, dreary, and down.

If you repeatedly find yourself feeling in the doldrums after spending much of the day behind your desk, it may be time to get outside and soak up some sunlight. Spending a few minutes in bright, natural light can elevate your mood and re-energize you for the rest of the day.

Take a Stand

Oftentimes, we spend much of our waking hours hunched over a keyboard, staring at a computer screen. No wonder your shoulders and backs are killing you. Sitting too long also leaves you feeling listless. Simply standing up can make you feel more alert and awake. Take a moment to stretch.

Walk around for a few minutes. You'll get your circulation going and help refocus your mind to the task at hand. Some people also swear by the benefits of a standing desk, especially one that lets your alternate between sitting and standing.

Hang Out with High-Energy People

Did you know you can "catch" emotions and behaviors from the people you hang out with? The phenomenon is known as social or emotional contagion, and it basically means that we are influenced by the outlook, moods, and demeanor of the people we surround ourselves with, including our co-workers and friends.

Be aware of how those around you may be influencing you. If you're constantly feeling down and blue when you hang out with certain people, maybe it's time to find a more positive, up-beat group to spend time with.

Mind Your Posture

Your mom always told you to sit up straight; it turns out she was onto something. Studies have shown that having good posture and sitting with a straight spine can give you an instant boost, lift your mood, and make you feel more enthusiastic and excited.

Sitting upright while working can also help improve your memory and your ability to recall information. Meanwhile, those who sit slumped over are more likely to feel passive, dull, and sleepy. So, shoulders back, head up. You'll feel better.

Get More Restful Sleep

Not getting enough sleep can leave us sluggish and exhausted. But feeling stressed can also make it difficult to fall asleep, leading to insomnia. Try destressing before bed to maximize your relaxation and help your body and mind unwind and calm down from the day.

Take time before bed to decompress with a warm bath or shower, listen to relaxing music, do some light stretching or deep breathing exercises, sip some herbal tea, or read something that is calming for a few minutes.

Cue Your Playlist

If you're hitting the gym, chances are you've got a workout playlist that keeps you moving. But music is something you can use at any time to increase your motivation and help you feel energized. Music releases endorphins, and fast-paced songs can increase your heartbeat and alter your mood, making you feel more alert and raring to go.

Try listening to upbeat music when you feel like you need a pick-me-up. If you need a break, try listening to some of your favorite songs to get your juices flowing. But research also shows that lyrics can be distracting, so if you're doing something that requires a lot of focus, opt for mellow, instrumental music at a lower volume.

CHAPTER

6

THE HEALTH REFLEX

So far, we've covered the first two points on our STARS model, the S or Sense of Purpose, and the T, which stands for the Traits of the top 2%. Now let's move over to the next point on the STARS model: Attitudes. We've identified four attitudes that people who are the highest-paid, highest-profile people in their industries have in common. And in this chapter, we're going to cover the first one, which is Healthy Habits.

It's not an exaggeration to say that the difference between life and death is often your attitude. Two people can come down with the same disease at the same time, and one of them will thrive while the other doesn't survive. The difference is their attitude. One of them had the attitude, "Why me?" And the other one had the attitude, "OK, so it's me. What is the good thing in this situation?"

HOW DO YOU DEFINE "HEALTHY"?

When you think of who is in the top 2% as far as physical health goes, your mind probably goes to a professional athlete. Clearly, athletes are in the top 2% of their professions and are the highest-paid, highest-profile people in their fields. But are they all in the top 2% of HEALTHY people?

Not always. Just because you're a professional athlete doesn't necessarily mean that you're one of the STARS when it comes to health.

Dr. Michael Selden wrote the study that he presented at the American College of Gastroenterology's 74th Annual Scientific Meeting in San Diego in 2009. He found that the link between how we perceive body size and health was a key indicator of our overall health attitude:

"We expect professional athletes to be in peak physical condition given the demands of their jobs and the amount of time they spend exercising heavily. However, there does not seem to be a complete protective effect of exercise, particularly among the larger athletes—football linemen. Instead, the impact of their sheer size may outweigh the positive benefits of exercise to mitigate their risk for cardiometabolic syndrome, fatty liver disease, and insulin resistance."

So just because you're a big, muscular athlete doesn't mean you're automatically healthy. But what about the other end of the spectrum? What about those who participate in sports where it's better to be lean, like ballet, figure skating, or gymnastics. Are leaner athletes healthier?

Again, the answer is not always yes. In an article on the psychology department web page of Vanderbilt University, Ana Cintado says:

Eating disorders are especially common among athletes because the pressure of the sport environment frequently precipitates the onset of these problems. In this population, certain compulsive behaviors, such as excessive exercise and restricted eating patterns, are seen as acceptable, and pathogenic methods of weight control are often introduced. In addition, concern about body size and shape is increased because of the "social influence for thinness [from coaches and peers], anxiety about athletic performance, and negative self-appraisal of athletic achievement." Finally, the competitive nature of sports reinforces characteristics, such as "perfectionism, high-achievement motivation, obsessive behavior, control of physique, and attention to detail." Most successful athletes are more determined and more disciplined than the average individual. They often set very high goals for themselves and work extra hours each day to reach them. These same attributes, however, can lead to eating disorders and are often found in anorexic and bulimic patients.

Being thin isn't necessarily a good thing, either. So, if you're not supposed to be too big or too thin, what ARE you supposed to be? Of course the answer that comes to mind is "just right." But how is "just right" determined if it's not body weight? One answer is body FAT. So really, the key has less to do with body WEIGHT and more to do with the amount of body FAT. You've got to have enough body fat to fuel your performance, but not so much that it's going to slow you down or start causing health problems.

FOCUS ON OVERALL HEALTH

So far we've looked at professional athletes who are putting their health in danger because they're too big or too thin. But what about athletes who are healthy? What do they do?

Should everyone go out and become a vegan? No, not at all. We've looked at professional athletes who believe that being overweight or obese will help them perform better. We've looked at other athletes who develop eating disorders because they believe that the thinner they are, the better they will perform. And why do these athletes develop these beliefs? Because they have people around them telling them that this is so. Our culture tells people that they have to eat meat or weigh a certain number to be healthy. And then people mindlessly follow. "Oh, I'm supposed to eat low-fat food? OK, I'll stock up on low-fat cookies, cakes, muffins, and breads and then I'll be healthy." "Wait, carbs are bad? OK, I'll cut out eating carbohydrates and live on bunless bacon cheeseburgers." "Animal products are bad for me? Fine. I'll be a vegetarian. Soda and french fries are vegetarian foods. I'll just eat that."

See? It's not about WHAT you eat, per se. It's about your attitude. It's about thinking for yourself instead of listening to what the so-called experts tell you to do. Does anyone really need to be told that living on fast-food and eating a diet of processed food is bad for them? Do we really doubt that eating a diet that's based on whole foods, fruits, and vegetables is good for us? Do we really need experts to tell us this? No. It's about listening to your body and developing habits for health that work with YOUR life and YOUR body. Because it's not about eating a certain way or going on a diet so that your body can perform in a sport or contest. It's about valuing your body as the vehicle that gets you to your goals. Your body is, in essence, the rocket ship that will get you to the STARS. And like any NASA engineer will tell you, you've got to maintain that rocket so that it will perform at its best.

You might be wondering why we titled this chapter "The Health Reflex." The reason is that the people who are in the top 2% have healthy habits that are like a reflex. For them, making healthy choices is as automatic as breathing or lifting their hand from a hot stove. If they go to a party, for example, they're not thinking, "Oh, those cream puffs look delicious. I want them, but oh . . . I shouldn't. I'm trying to be good on my diet." No. For the STARS, healthy choices are a reflex. They walk up to the buffet, put some fruit on their plate, and walk back to the table. It's automatic. They don't have to "try" to be healthy. They just are.

THE QUICKFIT PROGRAM™

So how can you do that? How can you use your body as a vehicle that will propel you to the top 2% of your field? We've developed a program to help you do this. It's called the QuickFit Program™. The

QuickFit Program™ is a complete mind, body, and spirit wellness program that will get you thinking about your health in terms of your whole LIFE instead of how you look in a bathing suit or how you perform in sports. This program will get you thinking about health as a practice, not a destination. That's an important distinction.

The QuickFit Program™ is a set of HABITS. That means that these are thoughts and behaviors that you integrate into your daily life. It's not something that you do for six weeks or six months until you hit a goal and then you stop. The people who are the highest-paid, highest-profile people in their industries have made health a HABIT in their daily life.

So, let's talk about some habits you'll want to address. If you're doing anything to excess, quit or cut back. There's a difference between having a beer with dinner and having a six-pack while you watch the game. You don't need the experts to tell you that you shouldn't be drinking six beers at a time. Develop a different habit for what you're drinking while watching TV.

What about soda? Do you need to eliminate that? The answer depends on you. If you're one of the millions of Americans who are drinking 54 gallons of soda a year, clearly you need to cut back. If you have a small soda once or twice a month when you're at a restaurant, you're fine.

How about sodium? We've all heard the statistics that say we're eating too much sodium. So, should YOU cut back on sodium? Maybe, maybe not. It depends on you.

The rationale for universal sodium restriction rests on a string of loosely related statistics:

- One in three American adults has high blood pressure, which is a major risk factor for stroke and death.
- The risk of high blood pressure goes up parallel to salt intake.
- The average intake of sodium is about 3,500mg per day. (The recommended intake is 2,300mg for healthy individuals and 1,500mg for those at risk.)

Based on this, the reasoning is that getting everyone to eat less salt will reduce the incidence of high blood pressure, thereby reducing strokes and death. But obviously, we're "treating" a lot of people who don't need it in order to get at those who do. Even among those with high blood pressure, only about 60 percent are salt-sensitive. For the other 40 percent, reducing sodium does little to correct high blood pressure. And some people have LOW blood pressure. What about them? Should they be reducing sodium, too? Or increasing it? Again, the answer depends on your body.

We've already talked about body weight. We learned in this chapter that it's less about the number on the scale and more about your body-fat percentage. Too much body fat, and you're at a higher risk of disease. Too little body fat, and you're at a higher risk of other diseases. You've got to build a lifestyle around the habits that will help you keep your body-fat percentage within a range that is healthy for you.

Let's talk about exercise. The more exercise you do, the fitter you are, right? Not necessarily. You see, the body perceives exercise as a stress. After all, back in the cave days, the only time a person ran was when he was being chased by a bear. The body perceives this as stress! Does this mean that exercise is bad and we shouldn't do it? Of course not. But too much exercise can be as detrimental to overall health as too little exercise.

You see, the QuickFit Program isn't about following a set of guidelines about what to eat or drink or how much to exercise. It's about customizing a program that works for YOU and your situation. It's about having the attitude that your health is something that you're constantly improving and working on. No matter how fit or healthy you are, you've got to work on it every day.

And that's what this chapter has really been about. It's about maintaining a healthy attitude and finding a program that works for you—every day. It's about implementing healthy habits that will fuel your success, allowing you to reach the STARS. For when you're in the top 2% of your field, you have the greatest power to influence and inspire others.

In the next chapter, we'll get into the second Attitude in our STARS model, the attitude of Continual Learning.

ENTREPRENEUR FOCUS
Grow Your Business by Focusing on Personal Health

In 2018, Elon Musk famously said that people need to work "80 to 100 hours per week" if they want to change the world. His comments are a reflection of the view that it is not enough to work smart—you have to work hard, too.

Unfortunately for Mr. Musk, while working those kinds of hours helped him create successful businesses, they may take a terrible toll on his health and future ventures. Working 80-plus-hour weeks is not sustainable for most and leads to poor concentration and high levels of unsustainable stress.

From a health perspective, therefore, Musk is not a model for entrepreneurs to follow, and even he admits that. Entrepreneurs need to guard against personal health issues so that they can guide their businesses through tough times. Working long hours is not out of the question, but those who go down that route need to offset it with behaviors that foster well-being.

Getting Enough Sleep Improves Productivity and Reduces Errors

Sleep experts recommend that we all get between seven and nine hours of sleep per night. If people get less than that, trouble can start.

A recent study from the RAND Corporation, for instance, found that lack of sleep causes the average person to lose around 11 days of productivity per year, translating to $2,280 in lost output. For high-value workers, such as entrepreneurs, this figure is likely *much* larger, given the repercussions of their decision making.

Furthermore, lack of sleep may lead entrepreneurs to make more errors (such as posting questionable tweets on Twitter). Studies show that sleep-deprived people are 20 to 30 percent more likely to make critical mistakes.

Eating a Healthy Diet Improves Mood and Enhances Output

Our culture tends to underplay the profound effect that what you eat has on health and productivity. But this isn't something lost on health authorities. The World Health Organization, for instance, indicates that eating a balanced diet raises productivity levels by around 20 percent—the equivalent of an extra day every week in the office.

The type of food you eat can also impact your mood. Researchers reporting in the *British Journal of Health Psychology* found evidence that eating more than seven portions of fruit and vegetables per day significantly improved participants' moods and better prepared them for the challenges of life.

Exercise Boosts Productivity and Improves Interpersonal Relationships

Top entrepreneurs around the world swear by their exercise routines, and this should come as no surprise. Data indicate that physical activity offers numerous benefits, including better mental well-being, improved overall health, and lower stress.

One study, for instance, found that worker productivity was an astonishing 72 percent higher on days when participants exercised compared to those on which they didn't. Another study found that implementing a "sit less, move more" policy reduced days lost due to lack of performance and improved interpersonal relationships.

Being Mindful Reduces Stress and Improves Decision-Making

Entrepreneurs often try to automate their personal lives so that they can dedicate their energies to their work. Taking this approach too far, however, can lead to undesirable unintended consequences, including a loss of focus, high stress levels, and poor decision-making.

Daily mindfulness, something practiced by everyone from Steve Jobs to Richard Branson, can help. A recent study from the University of California found that just two weeks of mindfulness training could boost focus dramatically. Another study from the University of Pennsylvania found that meditative practices reduced susceptibility to the "sunk cost fallacy" (when you continue a behavior as a result of previously invested resources)and helped foster clearer decision-making. And finally, research out of Johns Hopkins indicates that those who practice mindfulness experience a moderate but noticeable reduction in overall stress level.

Put on Some Music to Reduce Stress and Stay Focused

Listening to music in the office can have an extraordinarily relaxing effect on our brains by reducing stress and tension levels throughout the body. MusicDigi founder William Alfred confirms that "listening to your favorite music can help anchor you in the moment, letting you actually enjoy what you're doing, even if it's tedious or stressful. This helps you stay focused, motivated, and overall happier throughout your day."

Social Support Can Increase Happiness in Tough Times

Finally, entrepreneurs can improve their health and their businesses by seeking social support where necessary. Many of the world's top business leaders have a mentor, and research suggests that people who have good relationships with people both inside and outside the firm experience lower levels of workplace stress and higher perceived happiness.

Focusing on personal health, therefore, is not an option for entrepreneurs. It is an essential tool that allows them to improve their operations and make better decisions, allowing them to become the pillar of their organization and the person always there in the background who makes it thrive.

7

EVO LEARNING

I n this chapter we're going to cover the second Attitude that we've noticed among the highest-paid, highest-profile people in any industry—an attitude of Continual Learning.

Learning can happen at any age. Consider the man that many are calling the World's Oldest Blogger. His name is Randall Butisingh, and he wrote a personal blog until he was 97 years old. Here is what he said about learning. He was 97 years old when he wrote this:

My life was not planned. I followed wherever the current led. I found interest in whatever shore I was cast on by the waves of chance, and performed with interest and enthusiasm. My chief interests were health and strength of body and freedom of mind. I learnt many lessons along the way. . . . Up till now, I have followed no dream, but I have tried to do my best, many times blundering, with whatever came my way. I was pupil, fisher, crab catcher, laborer, pork knocker, teacher, lay reader, third class country cricketer, swimmer, acrobat, Welfare Officer, member and delegate of a Literary Institute, Chairman of an Indian Literary Institute, Hindi teacher, poet, journalist, Magazine editor and student of religion and philosophy. And now, nearing the end of my sojourn of my earthly existence, I am still seeking, still learning. My happiest moments are when I can help someone, when I can put a smile on someone's face or give someone hope.

What an amazing man! He clearly has lived a full and rich life. And he's the perfect illustration of the attitude we're talking about today—an attitude of continual learning.

Do you remember when you were a young child? You couldn't wait to learn new things. Perhaps you learned how to ride a bike, swim, play a sport, build a model airplane . . . you learned to cook, read, and write, maybe even play a musical instrument. As parents, we take our children to classes, lessons, and school. We give them religious instruction, tutoring, and teach them how to do things ourselves. And yet, what do we do for ourselves? What have YOU learned lately?

You see, learning doesn't only come in the form of school. An attitude of continual learning means that you're constantly learning new things. Now, you might be thinking, "I don't have time to be continually learning new things. Sure, I'd love to learn how to windsurf. But I'm too busy doing my J.O.B. and all the other things I need to get done in a day."

To that, we would answer what our friend Brian Tracy once said. He said, "Commit yourself to lifelong learning. The most valuable asset you'll ever have is your mind and what you put into it."

BENEFITS OF CONTINUAL LEARNING

So what are some of the benefits of continual learning? Well, research has shown that learning new things is extremely beneficial in a number of ways.

People who learn new things on a regular basis enjoy an improved memory, lessened risk of Alzheimer's disease, and stress reduction. In addition, relationships are improved because when you learn new things you often meet new people or become a better listener. You ask different questions. Creativity improves, too, because you're discovering a new way of doing things.

People who are continual learners do better at work. Here is a great example. A police officer in a major Metropolitan city was injured during an undercover sting operation. We'll call him Eric so we don't jeopardize his undercover status. Eric is injured and can't work the streets. He gets moved to a desk job, analyzing data. Now, Eric could have a bad attitude about it. He could be asking, "Why me? I don't want to be a data analyst. I didn't become a cop so that I could sit at a desk crunching numbers." But Eric has the attitude of the top 2% that we're talking about here. Eric is a continual learner. So Eric throws himself into his work and learns everything he can about data analysis. He even asks his supervisor to send him on a weeklong training out of state so that he can become certified in a particular technology. Eric gets the training and comes back to the job. Sure enough, there is a rash of bank robberies in the city, and Eric is the only one on the force who knows the information and technology that can be used to predict where the next robbery might occur. Suddenly, Eric is visible to the chief of police as well as several other key players on the force. As you can imagine, Eric's career possibilities just became much, much brighter. Now, if he wants to go back on patrol when he's well enough, he can. But, if he wants to, he can pursue another path as a data analyst. These options never would have been available to him if he'd closed his mind and his attitude toward learning something new.

It's like basketball legend John Wooden says, "It's what you learn after you know it all that counts."

LET GO OF EXCUSES

So what are some of the excuses we tell ourselves that keep us from being a continual learner? Not enough time is a big one. While there is a chapter on time management later in this book, let's just say that the "not enough time" excuse is really a matter of priorities. It's a matter of understanding the benefits of continual learning and then looking for opportunities to learn something new. We're not talking about enrolling in medical school here—unless you want to. We're talking about an attitude that every day brings new learning and being open to what life has to teach us.

What is another excuse that people use to keep themselves from learning? "I don't like school." Listen to what the founder of *Success* magazine, Orison Swett Marden, said before he died in 1924. "The Universe is one great kindergarten for man. Everything that exists has brought with it its own peculiar lesson. The mountain teaches stability and grandeur; the ocean immensity and change. Forests, lakes, and rivers, clouds and winds, stars and flowers, stupendous glaciers, and crystal snowflakes—every form of animate or inanimate existence, leaves its impress upon the soul of man. Even the bee and ant have brought their little lessons of industry and economy."

You don't ever need to step foot in a classroom to develop an attitude of continual learning. Hands-on learning and observation are among the most powerful tools for learning.

Here's another good example of an excuse that people use for not learning new things. "I am afraid of failure. I'll be embarrassed if everyone sees me fail." The truth is, those who say that should be MORE afraid of what people will think when they fail to learn. As William Pollard said in his book *The Soul of the Firm* (Zondervan, 1996), "Learning and innovation go hand in hand. The arrogance of success is to think that what you did yesterday will be sufficient for tomorrow." If you want to be one of the highest-paid, highest-profile people in your industry, you HAVE to keep learning new things.

As Nightingale-Conant author, Jim Rohn put it, "Learning is the beginning of wealth. Learning is the beginning of health. Learning is the beginning of spirituality. Searching and learning is where the miracle process all begins."

THE EVO LEARNING SYSTEM

Are you ready to become a continual learner? We've developed a process that will help you become a lifelong learner. It's called the EVO Learning System, and it covers the three main areas of learning: formal education or school learning; things you learn just for fun, like a hobby or a mental vacation from your life; and things that are related to your work or career. So, EVO Learning stands for Education, Vacation, and Occupation.

Education

Let's talk a little about the three kinds of learning. First, E, for Education. If you doubt the value of formal education, let me share some recent (2019) statistics from the National Center for Education Statistics. These stats represent the Annual Earnings by Educational Attainment. Some are higher, and some are lower. Are you ready? For 25- to 34-year-olds working full time, higher educational attainment equated with higher median earnings. According to the NCES, "in 2019 the median earnings of those with a master's or higher degree ($70,000) were 26 percent higher than the earnings of those with a bachelor's degree ($55,700), and the median earnings of those with a bachelor's degree were 59 percent higher than the earnings of those who completed high school ($35,000)." This is a little shocking, isn't it? You can have the same people, twins even. One becomes a doctor, and one drops out of high school. They could be equally wonderful people, great parents, and have the same talents and personality. But the one who has more formal education will be earning almost $104,000 than the other!

So, clearly, the more formal education you have, the more financially rewarded you will be.

Vacation

Let's move on to the next kind of learning in the EVO Learning System. V stands for Vacation. Now, you might think the word *vacation* means when you go away somewhere tropical and lie on a beach with a fruity drink in your hand. But we aren't using vacation to mean travel. We're using the word vacation as a derivative of the word *vacate*. As in "to leave." We're talking about the kinds of activities you do that let you leave your work or schooling behind. It's a hobby or an avocation that you do to relieve stress or increase pleasure.

Occupation

Finally, let's talk about the third kind of learning in the EVO Learning System. It's O for Occupation. This is learning you do to further your career. Now, we're not talking about getting additional training or certifications, although that's fine. The kind of learning we are talking about is an attitude of openness. It's about not becoming so engrained in your work that you lose sight of creative or new ways of doing things or of being.

THE FLEXBACK TECHNIQUE

Nightingale-Conant author Marshall Goldsmith is one of the few executive advisors who has been asked to work with more than 120 major CEOs and their management teams. In 2004 he was recognized by the American Management Association as one of 50 great thinkers and business leaders who have impacted the field of management over the past 80 years. Clearly, he is one of the highest-paid, highest-profile, top 2% management consultants in the world.

Marshall was a pioneer in the use of a 360-degree feedback technique within corporations to help leaders at all levels of management learn how to use feedback from their bosses, peers, and direct reports. But we know that not all our readers are in the corporate world, so we've created a learning technique that is based on the work of Goldsmith, but applies in any work situation. If you're a solopreneur, a freelance writer, a small-business owner, or a therapist, or you are a corporate employee, this technique can work for you. It's called The Flexback Technique.

To use The Flexback Technique, you want to identify the key stakeholders in your work. These are people who have an interest in your business. Of course, customers come to mind. But also think about anyone who is related to your work. So, if you're an artist, you might think of the suppliers that you use for your raw materials. If you have any employees, they are the stakeholders. If you have a boss, that person would be a stakeholder.

Then, you want to approach your stakeholders and ask their opinions about how you're doing. Depending on the dynamics of your work situation, you could do it face to face or through a survey. The size of your list will impact that decision, too.

Now, this is far more than a standard customer service kind of survey. You're going to be asking questions that go far deeper than "On a list from 1 to 5, how satisfied are you with my performance?" You see, every person you work with has something that they can teach you. If you open yourself up to the message, you will be a much richer person, both professionally and personally.

Asking the questions is only the first half of The Flexback Technique. One of the things Goldsmith teaches leaders is to set a specific date for follow-up. In other words, you contact the person again to let them know what the impact of their feedback was. So, for each person on your stakeholder list, you make a specific date and time to follow up with them. For example, you could circle back with colleagues a month or two after receiving feedback to let them know what steps you took to implement change and what the results of that change were.

You can use The Flexback Technique in your personal life, too. Goldsmith does this. Every year he has a one-on-one meeting with each of his children, his wife, his friends, and family. In the meeting, he asks them, "Is there anything you'd like me to do more of? Is there anything you'd like me to do less of? What is one thing you'd really like for me to understand?" And then he LISTENS. He doesn't argue, defend, or explain. He opens himself up to the learning that they have to give. And frankly, by doing this at home and at work, this is how Goldsmith got to be one of the most highly paid, high-profile management consultants in the world.

That attitude of openness is the one we're talking about here. It's an attitude of continual learning. Whether you're getting a formal education, you're vacating from your life in the form of a hobby, or you're learning in your occupation, an EVO learner is someone who is always growing.

In our next chapter, we'll cover the third attitude in our STARS model: being strategically content.

ENTREPRENEUR FOCUS
Learning the Agile Way

One of the critical concepts everyone is taught in Business 101 is to streamline your operation to provide more value to users. Should we apply that same "lean" approach to our knowledge acquisition and squeeze more value from what we learn. It's a method that experts call "agile learning," and it also entails unlearning information that is no longer useful.

Learning agility is a more dynamic and smarter approach, trimming the fat and leaving the most valuable information. So, when you forget for the umpteenth time where you left your keys, perhaps that's not a bad thing. Maybe you're just making room for more useful data.

To be competitive, entrepreneurs must be able to learn with agility so they can adapt and advance in an ever-changing marketplace. Studies have found that learning agility is even more important than job performance. Here are six strategies for developing your capacity for agile learning.

Make Reading Your Default Mode

A pillar of learning agility is continually consuming information, and there's no better way to do that than reading. Not only does it expand your vocabulary and introduce you to new subject matter, but reading can also help you discover new ways of thinking.

For a long time, I made excuses for not reading more material that didn't pertain to my work. I was trying to scale my startup and still spend time with my family. *Who can find the time?* But at a certain point, I started reading during the "between" times: between meetings, on the train, over breakfast, or even listening to audiobooks during my lunchtime walk. That way, there was no need to find the time—I already had it.

Everyone is busy. But if Mark Cuban reads three hours a day, and Bill Gates finishes one book a week, then I can, too.

Learn Deliberately

There are three types of learning: accidental, conscious, and deliberate. The first kind happens *to us*; for example, you're walking down the street and see a sign for a new streaming service. The second kind is when we learn but not necessarily purposefully, like via reading the paper or watching the evening news.

The third kind, deliberate learning, is when we're actively trying to acquire new information. Our attention is focused, and our thinking is sharp. And ultimately, we intend to incorporate this material into our existing framework and be able to access it later. To become an agile learner, it's important to make a habit of learning deliberately. And because only you know which lessons are most relevant to your work and your future, each individual's autodidactic path will be unique.

Learn in Short, Regular Intervals

It's crucial to set aside time for that deliberate learning every day, and a little bit goes a long way, especially if you make it a regular habit. Though knowledge workers spend an average of just five minutes on learning each day, experts recommend dedicating 30 minutes to an hour per day.

To make the most of your study session, entrepreneurs and *Harvard Business Review* contributors Josh Bersin and Marc Zao-Sanders recommend maintaining a to-learn list, advising: "Write down a list of concepts, thoughts, practices, and vocabulary you want to explore; bookmark them in your browser; and add them to your list. You can later explore them when you have a few moments to reflect."

Learning in small but regular allotments is effective because they are brief, and, therefore, sustainable, but also consistent, helping to continually cement recently acquired information.

Learn from Others with Experience

If you want to learn anything faster, start by tapping someone who has personal experience with the subject. And if they've mastered it, even better. Entrepreneur and author Tony Robbins captured this idea perfectly:

> *The fastest way to master any skill, strategy, or goal in life is to model those who have already forged the path ahead. If you can find someone who is already getting the results that you want and take the same actions they are taking, you can get the same results. It doesn't matter what your age, gender, or background is. Modeling gives you the capacity to fast-track your dreams and achieve more in a much shorter period of time.*

This "modeling" technique, as Robbins calls it, enables us to learn from the experience of others, including any mistakes, and save time in our own journey. Not to mention, it's more fun and energizing than learning alone.

Cross-Train between Subjects

In the past, people thought success came through specialization or achieving mastery in a single subject. As the saying goes: jack of all trades, master of none. That way of thinking is antiquated at best and self-defeating at worst.

Today, people are increasingly recognizing the value of becoming "expert generalists"—understanding the forest.

What's more, we learn better and with more agility when we can forge connections across boundaries and transfer knowledge from one subject matter to another.

Practice

Finally, like any skill, your capacity for agile learning will improve with practice. Forget the notion that some people are born better learners. As Dr. K. Anders Ericsson, a specialist in expert performance, explains: "People believe that because expert performance is qualitatively different from normal performance, the expert performer must be endowed with characteristics qualitatively different from those of normal adults. This view has discouraged scientists from systematically examining expert performers and accounting for their performance in terms of the laws and principles of general psychology."

With few exceptions (e.g., the height and ability to play basketball), most factors that determine our performance aren't genetically prescribed. Ericsson and colleagues argue that "the differences between expert performers and normal adults reflect a life-long period of deliberate effort to improve performance in a specific domain."

Similarly, your effort vis-à-vis learning should be deliberate. But don't consider it another task to add to your routine. Instead, think of agile learning as a lifestyle, one that will improve your business and hopefully enrich your life.

THE "READY, SET, LET GO" PROCESS

In this chapter we're going to talk about the third attitude in our STARS model, the attitude of being Strategically Content. What does the term *strategically content* mean? Let us share a parable with you that illustrates the attitude of being strategically content:

A shopkeeper sent his son to learn about the secret of happiness from the wisest man in the world. The lad wandered through the desert for 40 days and finally came upon a beautiful castle, high atop a mountain. It was there that the wise man lived.

Rather than finding a saintly man, though, our hero, on entering the main room of the castle, saw a hive of activity: Tradesmen came and went, people were conversing in the corners, a small orchestra was playing soft music, and there was a table covered with platters of the most delicious food from that part of the world.

The wise man conversed with everyone, and the boy had to wait for two hours before it was his turn to be given the man's attention.

The wise man listened attentively to the boy's explanation of why he had come, but told him that he didn't have time just then to explain the secret of happiness. He suggested that the boy look around the palace and return in two hours.

"Meanwhile, I want to ask you to do something," said the wise man, handing the boy a teaspoon that held two drops of oil. "As you wander around, carry this spoon with you without allowing the oil to spill."

The boy began climbing and descending the many stairways of the palace, keeping his eyes fixed on the spoon. After two hours, he returned to the room where the wise man was.

"Well," asked the wise man, "Did you see the Persian tapestries that are hanging in my dining hall? Did you see the garden that it took the master gardener ten years to create? Did you notice the beautiful parchments in my library?"

The boy was embarrassed and confessed that he had observed nothing. His only concern had been not to spill the oil that the wise man had entrusted to him.

"Then go back and observe the marvels of my world," said the wise man. "You cannot trust a man if you don't know his house."

Relieved, the boy picked up the spoon and returned to his exploration of the palace, this time observing all the works of art on the ceilings and the walls. He saw the gardens, the mountains all around him, the beauty of the flowers, and the taste with which everything had been selected. Upon returning to the wise man, he related in detail everything he had seen.

"But where are the drops of oil I entrusted to you?" asked the wise man. Looking down at the spoon he held, the boy saw that the oil was gone.

"Well, there is only one piece of advice I can give you," said the wisest of wise men.

"The secret of happiness is to see all the marvels of the world and never to forget the drops of oil on the spoon."

This parable perfectly illustrates the idea that we're talking about in this chapter. Those people who have made it to the top, who are in the top 2% and are the highest-paid, highest-profile people in their industries have learned one simple truth. It's not the destination that made them happy. It was the journey.

BE SELECTIVELY CONTENT

A lot of people say to us, "I'm confused. So many Nightingale-Conant programs are about goal setting and changing your life. But then there are also a lot of other programs that are about how to be happier and have less stress in the here and now. Which should I be focusing on? Goals for the future or being happy in the here and now?"

Aha! That is the age-old question in the field of personal development. Why would you want to change your life if you're happy with it? How can you balance the ideas of achieving goals and being happy now? It seems like a paradox, doesn't it?

People are used to being told to be content. But, paradoxically, successful people are never totally content—in many ways it is *discontent* with their current circumstances that drives them to achieve. And no matter how much these folks have achieved, they're never content to rest on their laurels. They're always looking for the next challenge. But that doesn't mean they're unhappy people.

The Top 2% of achievers are "strategic" about what they choose to be content about. They realize that there are certain situations, relationships, and circumstances where contentment is a virtue (such as playing with your children, tending to a sick parent, or listening to your spouse). However, they also realize there are areas where contentment is a vice (such as being content to stay in a dead-end job that offers no growth or challenge, where you just punch the clock day after day and "phone it in").

Another way you could look at it is being "selectively content." Think about your personal life. Which areas of your personal life would it be a VIRTUE for you to be content? In other words, is there something in your personal life that you're dealing with or that is difficult for you, but it would benefit you in the long run to be content? Again, maybe it's a relationship or some personal challenge you're facing, and it would be better for you if you could just learn to be content with the way things are.

Conversely, is there an area of your personal life where you're maybe overly content? Maybe there's an area of your personal life that would benefit from being a little LESS content and where contentment is a VICE. Maybe you're tolerating some things in your personal life that would be better for you to change?

Assess Your Level of Contentment

Let's do it for your professional life now. Which areas of your professional life would it benefit you to be more content? Maybe you have a boss that's a challenge, but you want to stay working for the organization. In this case, it would be a virtue for you to be more content.

What areas of your professional life, though, would benefit from you being LESS content? Are you tolerating some things professionally that it would be better if you didn't? In this case, being content with these things in your professional life is a vice.

The *Virtue or Vice?* exercise can help you determine in which areas of your life contentment is a virtue and in which areas it is a vice.

Benjamin Franklin summed up the idea of being strategically content perfectly when he said, "Content makes poor men rich; discontent makes rich men poor."

You have to be strategic about what you're content with.

Let's move on to another important attitude of the top 2% that relates to being strategically content.

Are you waiting to be happy? Have you said to yourself, "I'll be so happy when I reach my goal weight?" "Yeah, I'd be happy if I had a million dollars and could quit this lousy job." Or maybe, "I'll be happy when I buy that car, a house, get my degree, get married, have children . . ." When does it stop? "I'll be happy when my kids start school, and I have more time. I'll be happy when the kids go to college. I'll be happy when I can stop paying for college. I'll be happy when I retire." There's not much time after that, is there? Can you imagine waiting until your 60s or 70s to be happy? Looking back on your life and feeling like you'd wasted it because you were waiting for a future time to be happy?

Don't do that! Being happy in the present moment doesn't mean that you don't have goals. In fact, being happy in the present moment is a PRE-REQUISITE for achieving your goals. As one of our personal coaches here at Nightingale-Conant tells clients, "The seeds of your future happiness are present in your life today. It's up to you to shower them with attention so that they grow."

READY, SET, LET GO

To that end, you can identify the major goals in the core areas of your life and then see where, in your present life, the seeds of those goals are. For example, let's say you want to get an expensive car. You might be going around saying, "I can't wait until I get rid of this crappy car and can get my dream car." Instead of waiting to be happy about your car, you have to focus on the good things about the car you already have. What's good about your car? You might say, "Well, it works. And it's paid off. And it fits everyone in the family." So, you shift your thinking from hating your current car to appreciating it. Does this mean you don't want a different car? No. But being strategically content means that you're happy with what you have while you're striving for more. It's a fundamental attitude shift.

So, how can you become strategically content? We've developed a process that will help you balance out the actions of striving for goals with being content in your present life.

The Ready, Set, Let Go process covers the three elements of being strategically content. You have to get *Ready* to establish a goal and plan for it. You have to get *Set* and take the actions necessary to achieve the goal. And then you have to *Let Go* and detach from the outcome. This last step is often the hardest one for a lot of people, but it's also the most important. To use another gardening analogy, it's like when you plant a garden. You get ready by deciding which plants to plant, getting the soil and seeds, digging up the area, etc. Then, you get set. You plant the seeds in the ground and water them regularly. But, once this is done, you have to let go. You can't go out there and dig up the seed every day asking, "Is it a strawberry yet?" No, you have to get ready, get set, and then LET IT GO. Dreams and goals, like seeds, grow in their own time. Might as well be happy and enjoy yourself while they're growing.

Let's talk about how the Ready, Set, Let Go process would look in the different areas of your life.

Your Physical Health

To get ready, you want to clearly define what physical health means to you. Do you want to weigh a certain amount? Do you want to be able to achieve a physical goal, like running a marathon? Getting ready means clearly defining what the end result will look like.

Get set means that you start taking the actions that will lead you to that result. Focus on maintaining a balanced diet and exercise plan, for example.

And letting go means worrying less about how many pounds you're losing, which is a *result*, and instead focus on the thing you can control, which is what you eat and how much you move.

Relationships

OK, let's move on to relationships. What does the Ready, Set, Let Go process look like with relationships?

Getting ready means defining the kind of relationships you want to have. It's about setting a standard for how you want to be treated and how you want to treat others.

Getting set in this case means behaving in the relationship the way you want to be, regardless of how the other person is behaving. One of our Nightingale-Conant coaches recommends this exercise: "For one week, BE the kind of person you were when you first got married. If you used to make him breakfast every morning, do that now. Did you leave love notes in her bag? Do that again. It doesn't matter if the person deserves it, notices it, appreciates it . . . that's not relevant. You focus on being the kind of person in the relationship that YOU want to be, no holds barred, and report back to me in a week." Invariably, the client reports back that the relationship was much better that week and that he or she was much, much happier.

Letting go in this case means letting go of any expectations about how the other person will or won't behave. This is a tough one for many of us. "But if only he . . ." "I don't understand why she always . . ." Just let it go. Focus on the one thing you CAN control, and that is yourself.

Finances

Now, let's look at financial abundance.

Ready in this case would mean identifying how much money you would like to have. You should have a clear idea of how much money you want, and more important, WHY you want the money in the first place.

Getting set in the area of money would mean taking actions that lead to the generation of money. And, in most cases, that means focusing on creative ways to provide better service or to solve a problem that people are willing to pay for you to solve. Going after money directly is like trying to get a naked two-year-old child into the bathtub. The more you chase it, the more it runs screaming away from you. You have to get IT interested in what YOU are doing. So, in the case of the two-year-old, you're playing with a rubber ducky and bubbles, and the two-year-old comes up to you to see what's so fun. The energy of money is the same way. You have to be engaged in something interesting and worthwhile, and then it will come to you.

Finally, letting go in the area of money means just that—let go. Don't be so determined that your idea or your way to earn money is the only way it's going to happen. Be open to another way to receive the things that you want. Don't be all stressed out about "Why hasn't it happened yet?" Let go, focus on doing what you do and enjoying it, and wait for life to bring you the things that you established in the Get Ready stage of the process.

Flugelhorn jazz player John DePaola says it this way, "Slow down and everything you are chasing will come around and catch you. "

And the best part is, while you're rising to the STARS and becoming one of the highest-paid, highest-profile people in your industry, you'll gain one thing that money can't buy—happiness.

In our next chapter, we'll cover the fourth and final attitude in our STARS model: Self-Discipline.

ENTREPRENEUR FOCUS
Shift Your Contentment Mindset

Happiness is overrated.

Don't get us wrong, the "pursuit of happiness" is very quotable. It sounds great and looks great on paper—especially when that paper happens to be the Declaration of Independence, which is where the phrase can be found and was signed into existence by our forefathers.

However, it's difficult to ignore that the Founding Fathers linked happiness to external conditions, given that their concept of happiness was intrinsically connected to the pursuit of an unsecured future that promised better prospects than the present.

Based on that definition, it seems that the pursuit of happiness has high variability and volatility based on a bunch of subjective, external factors.

Our western society and capitalist system is geared toward an aggressive pursuit—perhaps more commonly known as the Rat Race—where happiness is linked to the pursuit of a certain job title, salary, house or car model, graduate degree, or any other number of random boxes that need to be checked to solve the happiness calculus.

Perhaps a more meaningful and achievable goal is "life, liberty, and contentment."

Happiness and contentment are quite different. Contentment suggests a stable and unmoving state of being that is linked to internal factors rather than external circumstances.

But contentment requires intentional, directed effort. Here are five steps that anyone can take toward that goal.

Community

We all have an internal need for the connection and relationship that can be found in a community where we are welcome and accepted, just as we are. That community might be in the workplace, but probably not.

Take a risk and volunteer at a charity organization in your area. Join a neighborhood theater, music group, or a crew with Habitat for Humanity. Go to a local church, synagogue, mosque—or something else you believe in—that will allow you to connect with others. This is a critical step because it creates a necessary climate for the rest of the steps.

Relevance

Once you've found your "tribe" of motivated and like-minded individuals, engage in their collective activities, projects, or initiatives. The satisfaction and sense of completion when you accomplish something that matters will be intrinsically gratifying and rewarding, which are critical components of contentment.

Growth

This step can take several forms, but it basically comprises some type of learning or personal development that helps you grow mentally, emotionally, spiritually, or physically.

Each of those dimensions of our existence needs to be nourished to thrive. Even seemingly small advances in personal growth can have an outsized impact toward a contented life.

Sharing

Without sharing the things that you value most—your time, talents, and "treasures"—it's difficult to find contentment.

Whether through mentoring, philanthropy, or teaching, an important step toward being content is giving and sharing with others.

Gratitude

Having an "attitude of gratitude" seems easy, but it's not.

Many successful, driven individuals are rightly proud of their professional or personal accomplishments, but inner problems arise when they unconsciously forget or minimize the support they received along the way. They're setting themselves up for disappointment when they delude themselves into believing that they did it all on their own.

Nobody achieves anything meaningful without the help and support of others. Regularly acknowledging that support and expressing gratitude for it, helps condition the heart and mind for life-altering contentment.

Whether we know it or not, we all desire contentment. These steps can help anyone map a contented path in life.

Self-help experts from Abraham Maslow to Tony Robbins have advanced some variation of these basic human needs in the past, so there's nothing new here because these are universal aspects of the human condition.

But these are good reminders for anyone stuck in the Rat Race who's driven by our western culture and materialistic pursuits.

It's important to know that you can stop running after a happiness that always promises to be reached tomorrow, when you can instead choose contentment today.

THE MAP TO
THE STARS

In this chapter we're going to cover the last of the four attitudes on our STARS model—Self-Discipline.

Now, usually when you hear the words "self-discipline," you think of "making yourself do what you should do." There are hundreds of books, audio programs, classes, magazine articles, coaching programs, and the like that are all designed to get you to have more self-discipline. Here at Nightingale-Conant we have many valuable resources available that can help teach you *how* to do what you know you should do.

But in this chapter, we're going to look at the idea of self-discipline from a different perspective. We're going to look at self-discipline as an ATTITUDE rather than a set of behaviors. Here's a story that illustrates the difference:

A successful real estate agent was approached by a younger agent who worked at a competing firm. The younger agent said, "I'm sure you won't want to do this, but is there any way we could meet for coffee and you could share with me what it is that you do that makes you so successful?" The successful agent agreed without hesitation. They sat for two hours at a local coffee house, and the successful agent told his young competitor the many disciplines that he regularly used to become so successful. As they were leaving, the younger agent said, "Why did you agree to do this? Aren't you afraid that I'll use all your suggestions and take away your business?" To which the successful agent replied, "I'm not worried about that at all. Very few people are willing to do what I do to be successful."

Can you see the difference? The successful agent had an ATTITUDE of self-discipline, and the younger agent wanted to know the ACTIONS of self-discipline. And, of course, those actions are important, and we'll be covering most of them in some later chapters of this program. But for our purposes in this chapter, we want to look at self-discipline as an attitude.

Let's break down the words self-discipline. Obviously, the word "self" means you. The word "discipline," though, has many connotations. Many of them are negative. When your kids get into trouble you have to "discipline" them. Or discipline can be synonymous with the term self-control. All these definitions imply sort of a struggle or force. It's more about willpower and forcing yourself (or someone else) to do something you don't want to do.

But what is the root of the word "discipline?" It's the word "disciple." And the word disciple comes from the Latin word that means "learner." And in this sense, the word discipline means a field of study.

So, in this way, a person with self-discipline is someone who has an attitude of learning in their field of study. That's what self-discipline is! Being a disciple in your field.

What a difference that shift in definition makes! When you define self-discipline that way, you go from feeling like "Ugh, I have to have more willpower so that I can make myself do what I need to do," to feeling like "What can I learn today that will make me more successful in my field?"

THAT is the attitude of the highest-paid, highest-profile people in any industry. They don't have to MAKE themselves do things; they do things because they want to. And wanting to do those things comes from an attitude of wanting to master one's discipline.

THE MAP

We've created a process that can help you access that inner disciple—the one who *wants* to do what he or she needs to do. It's called the Mental Alignment Process, or MAP for short. MAP can take you from you where you are now to where you want to be and help keep you motivated and on course even when obstacles arise.

In a previous chapter, we discussed the fact that the journey to the top of your field or industry is just as valuable as the destination. In fact, Earl Nightingale used to say, "Success is the progressive realization of a worthy goal." So, this metaphor of a journey toward your worthy goal of being one of the highest-paid, highest-profile STARS in your industry is a valid metaphor.

So, what do you do when you travel on a journey? Of course, you first identify your destination. A trip to Hawaii is going to require a different journey than a trip to Maine. Therefore, first, you need to decide where you want to go.

Then, you have to decide when you want to start. Not all journeys have the same time frame. If you're planning a bigger journey, it may take some time for you to embark because you'll need to gather together more resources. If the journey will be shorter, for, say, a smaller goal, the time frame will be sooner. So, first you decide where you want to go, then you decide when you want to start the journey.

Notice that we're not talking about planning when to ARRIVE at your destination. You have less control over that than you might imagine. Obstacles and detours will come your way that will delay you.

Next you want to identify your route. How will you travel from point A to point B? For any given destination, in both the travel sense and the goal sense, there are almost an infinite number of ways to get there. So, you have to decide which route you'll take. Don't worry too much about choosing the RIGHT way to get there, however. You'll probably end up taking a slightly different route than you planned anyway. But it doesn't always matter HOW you get to your destination, or even WHEN you get there. It just matters that you get there.

The next thing you want to do when you're planning a journey is prepare. You have to gather all the resources you'll need on your journey. You'll need to prepare yourself physically, mentally, and even spiritually. But don't spend too much time preparing. You don't need to overpack, so to speak. You can find the resources you need along the way.

Start Your Journey

OK! So now it's time to embark on your journey. You're all ready to go, you've got your route mapped out, you know where you're going, and it's finally time to start.

It's exciting! We've all had the experience of starting on a journey and know the exciting feelings and thoughts that go along with starting something new. You're happy, you're smiling, and you are anticipating a smooth journey.

Inevitably, though, on both a physical journey as well as our metaphorical one, the excitement wears off. You've left the comfort zone of home, and a part of you wants to go back. You're in unfamiliar territory, and you might even make a wrong turn or two. What are you going to do? If you come upon a roadblock in your journey, you've got two choices. You can turn back, or you can find another way.

So, find another direction. If you have to turn back or go home for a short while, that's OK, too. Sometimes we pick the wrong time to start out on a journey, or we don't have the resources we need, and it's just not worth it to keep going. Does that mean you'll NEVER get there? No. It just means that it might not have been the right time.

But what if you don't want to turn back? What if getting to your destination is more important than any obstacle that comes your way? Then, yes, you have to find another way. And if that doesn't work out, then you find yet another way. There are almost an infinite number of paths you can take to get to any destination.

So, you're going along and taking detours and going around roadblocks. What effect is that going to have on your journey? It's going to add on some time to how long you thought it was going to take. Remember, you can't really control WHEN you get to your destination, but you can control that you get there.

But there's no need to rush. The journey is what matters. So, enjoy it. Take the time to appreciate the beauty of the experiences you have along the way.

THE MAP IN ACTION

Another thing Earl Nightingale said is "All you need is the plan, the road map, and the courage to press on to your destination."

The metaphor of the journey has all the elements of MAP. And these elements are what will help you realign with your goals when you get off track. They are the key to developing the self-discipline you need to reach the top 2%. Here are the elements of MAP. They are:

- Choosing your destination
- Deciding when to start
- Determining your route
- Preparing for the journey
- Embarking on the journey
- Identifying obstacles and roadblocks
- Deciding whether to turn back or press on
- Choosing another path
- Staying the course
- Celebrating your arrival

Whenever you find your motivation for the journey lagging, go back to this process, and see where you are. Again, you will be creating a physical MAP as part of this process, and you can pull it out and literally see where you are in reference to your goal.

What the MAP will do is help you to get mentally realigned with your destination. If you're feeling lost, you can look and see where you've come from and where you're going. It helps you stay focused on the big picture.

Let's use MAP on an example so you can see it in action. I'm going to choose one that millions of people are struggling with—weight loss.

Eric was an athlete in college. Because of his rigorous training schedule, he never had to worry about his weight. But after graduation, Eric got a desk job, got married, and had kids. The weight of his responsibilities soon became weight on his body. Before he knew it, Eric was 65 pounds overweight.

Eric decides to use MAP to help him achieve his goal of getting in shape. Here is how it looks:

First, Eric chooses his destination. That's a goal weight, but he also wants to measure his body-fat percentage, too.

Next Eric has to decide when to start. He's taking a cruise for his wife's 30th birthday next month and figures he should probably wait until after that. Then, he'll be able to focus on his diet and exercise plan without distraction.

To determine the best route to weight loss, Eric reviews various diet plans. He decides to go on one of those commercial weight-loss programs where they give you the food.

To prepare for the journey, Eric joins a gym, signs up for the diet program, drags out his old workout stuff, and signs up for a basketball league in his neighborhood. He uses MAP to plot out a physical map of his journey.

Things are going well for six weeks or so. Eric is feeling good, losing weight, and making progress.

One day, Eric gets called into the boss's office. The quarterly sales figures are down, and he's going to have to put some extra hours in at the office and start bringing work home. The basketball league is out. He tries to get to the gym before work, but he misses a few days. Next thing he knows, he gets sidelined by the flu.

Eric is frustrated. The last thing he wants to do is eat his prepared diet food. He wants comfort food. He wants to sit on the couch with his wife and watch prime-time TV like he used to. Eric has to decide whether to turn back and try the journey again at a later time or press on.

Eric pulls out his MAP and looks at how far he's come. He realizes that this is only a roadblock. Eric really does still want to get to his destination. But he sees that he's going to have to choose another route to get there.

So, he goes online and finds another diet plan that allows him to eat his own food. He gets an exercise machine and a TV with a DVR for his home office so he can watch TV and exercise when he has to bring work home.

Of course, this isn't the only obstacle Eric faces. But every time he starts to lose his sense of discipline, he takes out his MAP and uses it as a visual reminder of how far he's come, where's he's going, and how much closer he is to his goal than he feels.

Soon, because he stayed the course, Eric achieves his weight-loss goal. It's time to celebrate and settle in before Eric moves on to use MAP on another goal.

MAP can be the tool that helps you stay mentally aligned with your goals. It can help you stay focused on having an attitude of learning, asking "What needs to change so I can reach this goal?" It's about staying the course until you become one of the STARS.

In our next chapter, we're moving on to the next point on our STARS model—rapport with others. We're halfway through!

ENTREPRENEUR FOCUS
Eight Ways to Focus on Your Goals

Accomplishing a goal can be hard work. Even if a project is something you are passionate about and want to complete, distractions, such as social media, doubts, and other tasks, can make it nearly impossible to concentrate on it.

But don't fret. Check out these eight steps to help you prioritize and clear your mind.

1. *Stop multitasking.* Instead of trying to do a million things at once, take a step back and tackle one task at a time. And while your inclination might be to start your day with busy work—like checking emails—and then move onto to the harder things, you should try to get your brain moving by challenging yourself with a bigger, more creative endeavor first.

2. *Block out your days.* A good way to hold yourself accountable when it comes to quieting the noise all around you is to specifically block out time in your day—maybe it's 30 minutes or an hour—to spend on a project. Color-code your calendar or set a timer to make sure you are accomplishing the goal at hand.

3. *Get your blood pumping.* You can't focus if you are stuck inside and staring at a screen all day. Turn off your computer and phone, and go for a walk for 20 minutes. The fresh air and the movement will clear your head. Also, make sure that you're drinking enough water and getting enough rest.

4. *Help your technology help you.* A platform like RescueTime, a software that runs while you work and shows you how you are spending your day, could help you understand why something is taking longer to complete than it should. Options like Cold Turkey, Freedom, and Self-Control block out the internet entirely to keep you off Facebook when you should be meeting deadlines.

5. *Meditate.* Get a recommendation for a yoga or meditation class, or even make it an office outing so everyone gets some time to quiet their minds. Or look online for a plethora of apps and platforms whose stock in trade is mindfulness, like Meditation Made Simple, Calm, and Headspace. For slightly more of a monetary investment, you could look into wearable tech like Thync, a device that produces electrical pulses to help your brain decrease stress.

6. *Change up what's in your headphones.* While background noise might help block out a loud office or construction outside your window, you need to be careful that what you are listening to isn't distracting you more. Music with lyrics can sap your focus

from the task in front of you, so consider trying classical or electronic music instead. Or use a playlist that is familiar to you, so you aren't tempted to turn all your attention to the new sound.

7. *Streamline your communication.* If you find that all your focus gets trained on getting your inbox down to zero, think about how you can get yourself out from under a relentless deluge of email. Ask yourself and your colleagues to think about whether this conversation would be most effective through email, on the phone, or in person. Taking five minutes to walk over to someone else's workspace will save you the time and energy invested into a redundant email chain and clarify how you want to attack a problem more quickly.

8. *Find an environment with the right kind of noise.* To be the most effective, you need to strike a delicate balance between too much noise and total silence. According to David Burkus, an associate professor of leadership and innovation at Oral Roberts University, "Some level of office banter in the background might actually benefit our ability to do creative tasks, provided we don't get drawn into the conversation. Instead of total silence, the ideal work environment for creative work has a little bit of background noise. That's why you might focus really well in a noisy coffee shop, but barely be able to concentrate in a noisy office."

10

THE LASTING LEGACY PROCESS

We're now moving on to the next point in our STARS model: the R, which stands for Rapport. The word rapport is a French word that means a sense of mutuality and understanding—harmony, accord, confidence, and respect underlying a relationship between two persons. There are five rapport qualities in our model: being legacy-minded, demonstrating effective communication, being service-oriented, and having fulfilling relationships. In this chapter, we're talking about the first rapport quality: being legacy-minded.

You might be wondering what leaving a legacy has to do with rapport with other people. After all, a legacy is something you leave after you die. But for those people who are the highest-paid, highest-profile and in the top 2%, they're always thinking about making an impact. They're thinking about making change in a way that will last beyond their individual lives. And they also know that it's your relationship with other people and the impact that you have on them when you're alive that defines the legacy you leave once you're gone.

Roger Ebert began his career as a professional critic in 1967, writing for the *Chicago Sun Times*. In 1975, he branched out into TV with a weekly film review show. He and his first co-host, Gene Siskel, coined the phrase "two thumbs up" to indicate a movie that both critics liked. Gene Siskel died in 1999 and was replaced with fellow *Chicago Sun Times* reporter Richard Roeper. In 2002, Roger Ebert developed thyroid cancer and had numerous surgeries in an attempt to save his life. During the surgeries, he lost his lower jaw and, therefore, his ability to speak. The surgery left his face extremely disfigured and required the use of a computerized voice to speak the words that used to flow effortlessly from his mouth.

Such circumstances might cause a man to withdraw in a world of silence and solitude. Instead, when asked about his decision to return to the limelight, Ebert remarked, "We spend too much time hiding illness."

Instead, Ebert committed himself to leaving a new legacy—the perfection of computer voice technology. In 2011, Roger Ebert "spoke" at the TED conference in Long Beach, California, with the assistance of his wife, Chaz, physician Dean Ornish, musician John Hunter, and a computerized voice. He told the packed auditorium, "For most of my life I never gave a second thought to my ability to speak. It was like breathing. . . . In those days I was living in a fool's paradise."

In the months that followed the loss of his voice, Ebert grew frustrated as he explored different ways to communicate. Because he'd had a career on TV, he had many, many hours of his natural voice on audio. He sent them to a Scottish company, which developed a computerized speech program from the recordings of Ebert's own voice, and he played it to the TED audience. While it did bear the most resemblance to his original voice, it still sounded stilted and unnatural. But Ebert was committed to being the public face for those with speaking disabilities. He said, "Because of the digital revolution, I have a voice, and I do not need to scream."

Roger Ebert is the perfect illustration of a key point in our discussion of being legacy-minded. In his career as a movie reviewer, he thought his legacy was going to be in the area of movie reviews. Perhaps he thought his greatest contribution would be the "two thumbs up" concept. And he was definitely a significant influence in popular culture. But then he became ill and his ability to speak was taken away. As he put it, "All my life I was a motor-mouth. Now I've spoken my last words, and I don't even remember, for sure, what they were."

Ebert, who died in 2013, may not have been able to leave his legacy any more using words. But he still left a legacy. Being legacy-minded means staying open to the meaning of your life and thinking about the impact it will have on others, and the world at large.

LASTING LEGACIES QUIZ

Can you guess who these famous "lasting legacy" stories are about?

This first person was born in 1901 in Chicago, Illinois. At 16 years old, he joined the Red Cross. Throughout his life he was constantly sketching and drawing. In 1928, he made the world's first silent cartoon from one of his sketches. He went on to become a household name. Do you know who this person is?

It's Walt Disney. Walt Disney clearly had a great impact on the world. People from all over the world come to visit his creations and ideas. Walt Disney World Resort is the most visited recreational resort in the world. Through his movies, and other contributions too numerous to mention, his legacy will never die and the name Walt Disney will always be a part of American society.

All right, let's do another one. Whose legacy is this?

This man started his career as a Navy pilot in 1949. In 1955 he became a test pilot for the Lewis Flight Propulsion Laboratory. From there, he went on to take a job at a government agency in Houston, Texas, that would change human history forever. Can you guess who it is?

It's Neil Armstrong, the first person to set foot on the moon. His famous words were "One small step for man, one giant leap for mankind."

Are you ready for another one?

This person was born in 1942 in Louisville, Kentucky. He dropped out of high school and tried to join the military but failed the written exam because of his poor spelling. Then, in 1964 this man became a Muslim and changed his name. In 1967, he refused to be drafted into the U.S. military based on his religious beliefs, and he was arrested and found guilty. He appealed, and it took four years for his conviction to be overturned. The man went on to become a professional athlete and was named Sportsman of the Century by *Sports Illustrated* magazine. Do you know who I'm talking about?

It's Muhammad Ali, the man who defeated every top heavyweight in his era. But even more than his boxing legacy, Ali is also known as a civil rights activist and as a public face, alongside Michael J. Fox, for Parkinson's disease.

YOUR UNINTENTIONAL LEGACY

You may not have thought of it this way, but everyone leaves a legacy. Whether you're thinking about it or not, the people around you are watching how you live your life and are learning from it. Good or bad, your actions and words are defining how you are remembered. We call this your Unintentional Legacy.

Your Unintentional Legacy has the power to completely destroy your positive contributions. One great example of this is former American President Richard Nixon. During his presidency, he effectively ended American involvement in the unpopular Vietnam War. He opened diplomatic relations with the People's Republic of China, implemented sweeping environmental reforms that are still in place today, and many other positive contributions. But what is the first thing that comes to mind when you hear the name Richard Nixon? It's probably the phrase "I am not a crook." His Unintentional Legacy was that he resigned from the presidential office because he was about to be impeached. History doesn't remember him for the positive contributions he made. We remember him for his Unintentional Legacy.

What is your Unintentional Legacy? What impact are you having on the people around you? To figure it out, you can perform a personal assessment called the Impact Survey. To complete the Impact Survey, write down the names of the last ten people who came to your office, called you on the phone, or instant messaged, texted, or emailed you. Don't include people who just forwarded you jokes or something, but the last ten conversations you had. Next to each of their names, write down what it is they wanted. Did they want your insights on a problem they're having? Did they look to you for support or an emotional pep talk? Were they contacting you to resolve a conflict or to get them some information? Maybe they needed you to give them a firm answer for something. Next to their names, write down what they wanted.

Now, place a check mark next to the people who contact you on a regular basis for a similar issue.

What are the themes you see? Are you a creative problem-solver? Are you an emotionally supportive friend or colleague? Perhaps you're decisive and help people make decisions. The Impact Survey can give you some insight into the role you play in people's lives.

THE LASTING LEGACY PROCESS

Now it's time to move on to your Intentional Legacy. This is, of course, the legacy that you INTEND to leave. It's something you've thought about. The idea of creating a formal statement of your legacy comes from the book *Your Leadership Legacy* (Harvard Business Review Press, 2006) by Robert Galford and Regina Fazio Maruca. Their core idea is that your legacy is defined by how others approach work and life as a result of having worked and known you.

To make your legacy Intentional, we have come up with a three-step process called the Lasting Legacy Process.

Step 1: The LegaSEE Exercise

The first step in the Lasting Legacy Process is something called the LegaSEE exercise The exercise is based on the principles of NLP or neurolinguistic programming. The LegaSEE exercise is designed for you to create what you want your Intentional Legacy to be. But instead of picking something externally, the LegaSEE exercise allows you to seek the answers from within your mind and align the various parts of your mind with the legacy you wish to leave.

To do the LegaSEE exercise, you'll need to have a blank wall you can look at. If you can take down any pictures or items on the wall, that's good. If not, just pretend they're not there as you do this exercise.

Sit in a chair facing the wall and think about one quality you'd like to leave as part of your Intentional Legacy. For the purposes of our example, we'll pick compassion for others.

Now, looking at the wall, imagine that it is divided into six visual spaces. Each space will contain one area in which you're going to think about expressing compassion for others. So, imagine that the wall has six separate areas on it.

Next, you're going to focus on each space and think about how you can express your value of compassion for others in that area. The first space is environmental. Ask yourself, "Where and when do I wish to express compassion for others?" Staring at the space on the wall, be aware of the thoughts that come to your mind.

Move your eyes to the next area—the behavior space. Ask yourself, "What behaviors will help me express compassion for others in those times and places?" Again, let the answers come to your mind while you're looking at the space on the wall.

Now, move to the capabilities space. Ask, "What capabilities will help me express compassion for others in the form of those behaviors in those places and times?" Think about that for a while.

Next, train your eyes on the beliefs and values space. Ask, "What beliefs and values will help me express compassion for others through those capabilities, in the form of those behaviors, at those times and places."

Then, focus on the next space, which is the identity space. Ask, "What kind of person has those beliefs and values? What kind of person expresses compassion for others?"

Finally, move on to the last space. Ask, "What is my legacy in terms of compassion for others?"

Take some time to quietly reflect and notice any new ideas or insights that come to your mind. Then, close your eyes and imagine moving through the rest of your life expressing the value of compassion for others in the way just envisioned. Take as much time as you need for this step.

Now, you can use the LegaSEE exercise for any value you want to incorporate into your Intentional Legacy.

Step 2: Your Legacy Letter

OK, now we're ready to move on to Step 2 of the Lasting Legacy Process. It's called Your Legacy Letter. A Legacy Letter is simply a formalized statement of the values, behaviors, and approaches to life that you wish those who you leave behind to carry on.

To create your Legacy Letter, you want to spend some time reflecting on your life thus far. Think back to your childhood and teenage years. What values were you raised with? How did your life feel then? Are there things you wish to carry with you as you move forward? Are there things you wish to leave behind? Don't worry about thinking about specific events or well-formed memories. We're talking about impressions.

Move on to your life as a young adult. Recall your sense of things, isolated experiences, or even songs that come to mind from that time. What are the themes or characteristics of that period in your life? These are the things that have shaped you and still influence you.

In some sense, you're looking for what your Unintentional Legacy has been up to this point.

Everyone has stories or impressions in their personal history that represent your values and beliefs. So, spend the time to mine the data of your personal history banks for memories, impressions, ideas, thoughts, and the like.

Next, find the themes. Sort your thoughts into three headings: Characteristics, or who you are; Values, or what you hold in high esteem; and Manifestations, things that show up in your life. So, for Characteristics, look at who are you as a result of those earlier experiences? Determined, Persuasive? Resilient? For Values, ask, which ones mean the most to you? Honesty? Fairness? Which values do you respect in others? And for Manifestations, look at how those characteristics and values show up in your life—either as blessings or challenges.

And then, finally, write the letter.

Step 3: Revisit

Step 3 in the Lasting Legacy Process is to make sure to revisit your Legacy Letter at least once a year. This will help you make sure that your Intentional Legacy is aligned with your Unintentional Legacy. Did you take a job, for example, which is leaving an Unintentional Legacy that goes against the Intentional Legacy you desire to leave?

U.S. Senator Paul Tsongas captured the essence of a legacy beautifully when he said, "We are a continuum. Just as we reach back to our ancestors for our fundamental values, so we, as guardians of that legacy, must reach ahead to our children and their children. And we do so with a sense of sacredness in that reaching."

In our next chapter, we're going to cover the second Rapport quality—effective communication.

ENTREPRENEUR FOCUS
Five Factors for Planning Your Entrepreneurial Legacy

In business today, disruption is the name of the game. Entrepreneurs are constantly looking for ways to shake things up, find new perspectives, and change the rules.

While carving out a place for yourself in the market is crucial, focusing only on your numbers sheet is a bit shortsighted. For entrepreneurs, the sign of true success isn't short-term profits— it's a lasting legacy. Now more than ever, entrepreneurs need to look forward to what their long-term impact on the world will be. Knowing what you'll be known and remembered for down the line, however, isn't always easy. If you're hoping to turn your present success into a future legacy, it's important to start thinking ahead today. Here are some key factors to keep in mind when planning your entrepreneurial legacy.

Relationships

Building positive relationships is already a key component of good business. Digital marketing firm RevLocal reports that companies can lose between 20 percent and 80 percent of their customers by not cultivating healthy relationships with them. Despite the money that can follow strong connections with people, the value of relationships extends far beyond the financial realm.

Relationships are one of the elements of your legacy that you can start working on immediately. When dealing with people in your circle, take some time to think beyond the short term. It can be easy to go days or weeks simply viewing people as co-workers, clients, or competitors; in fact, these people are the ones who have the biggest hand in shaping your legacy going forward. Ensure that you're connecting with those around you, showing them the side of yourself that you want to be remembered for.

That includes constantly setting others up for success. Ask what you can help with. Offer to make an introduction. Investigate partnerships that make sense for both you and your potential partner. The more connections you make, the more indestructible your value becomes, both personally and professionally.

Social Impact

Entrepreneurs want to make valuable, lasting investments, but the impact of those investments shouldn't just be financial. Investing in environmental, social, and developmental causes can not only earn you your investment back, but it can also promote important work the world over.

Socially minded investing is no longer the niche practice it once was. According to the investment experts at family office services provider Pathstone, impact-focused investing has increased rapidly in recent years, accumulating to a total of more than $30 trillion. Identify causes important to you before scouting for various businesses and organizations that turn those causes into valuable investment opportunities.

Thought Leadership

Some trailblazing entrepreneurs may make their mark through tech innovations, organizational reshuffles, or early industry investments, but the entrepreneurs who truly change the game are often the ones who bring entirely new ways of thinking to the table. Developing powerful examples of thought leadership is one of the most effective ways to share your vision with the world.

According to a survey from LinkedIn, 58 percent of respondents read one or more hours of thought leadership content every week. With numbers like that, writing content that embodies your unique perspective might well be the best way to reach the largest possible audience. As your reach expands, you're able to lead conversations, influence opinions, and introduce ideas that may disrupt your industry. Whether it's talking about your field's supply chain or questioning how your industry addresses issues like sexual harassment, you can attract attention from both industry heavyweights and potential superstars who can help your company build its legacy.

Long-Term Growth

In the cutthroat world of startups, an emphasis on short-term growth is often necessary just to stay afloat. While staying solvent in the near term is a valuable strategy for ensuring your business's success now, legacy-focused entrepreneurs need to have an eye on sustaining long-term growth as well. It's much more difficult for your business to carry a legacy if it doesn't last. Many businesses in that position become warnings for others, à la Kodak.

The toughest part of planning for long-term growth is that it can be nearly impossible to do in the early stages of your career. While making evergreen investments and expanding into rising sectors are good places to start, there's simply no way to know exactly what will guarantee your success down the line. Younger entrepreneurs should try to adopt certain habits that can lead to future growth. Predicting the next big thing may be difficult, but creating a hardworking mindset is a surefire way to rise to the top. Gut instinct may not be with you at every step, but working harder than the next person is always a good calling card.

Succession

The world of entrepreneurship may often feel dog-eat-dog, but young business leaders around the world are looking for guidance. A study from digital-finance platform Kabbage reports that more than 90 percent of small-business owners describe their mentors as having directly impacted the growth and profitability of their business.

The responsibility of the older generation of business leaders is to cultivate the next generation. Think of mentorship as a combination of the relationships and thought leadership above. By mentoring young entrepreneurs in your circle, you're ensuring that your way of thinking will live on. You're also promoting the success of those close to you. Done right, mentorship can be a way to secure a legacy for yourself while benefiting others in the process and developing your own succession plans. To keep your legacy going, you'll want to ensure you've developed the right talent with the right vision, and this kind of mentorship is key to doing so.

In uncertain times, the desire to ensure that your legacy will live on can be greater than ever. As difficult as it can be to see beyond the short term, entrepreneurs today need to be looking forward. The future of their business may well depend on it.

11

ADVANCED COMMUNICATION APTITUDE

In this chapter, we'll cover the second quality in our Rapport category—effective communication.

Here is an example of what we mean by effective communication. Let's consider several scenarios and see if you can tell what the other person wants you to do or say.

In the first scenario, you're in a conference room waiting for the CEO of the company to arrive. It's a large company, and you rarely have the opportunity to meet with him in a small-group setting. He walks in, sits down, looks around the room, fans his face with a folder, and says, "Does anyone else think it's hot in here?"

What's your first instinct? It's probably to get up and open a window or something. You understood that the boss wasn't actually asking if people agreed with him; he was looking for someone to solve the problem of the temperature of the room.

In the next scenario, your mother-in-law is coming to dinner. You and she don't get along all that well, although you really love your spouse and want to get along with your mother-in-law better. Your mother-in-law sits down at the dinner table, begins eating, looks directly at you, and says, "Does anyone else think it's hot in here?"

What's your first reaction here? You probably would perceive it as a criticism. You might open a window, but you also know that she's not asking if anyone agrees with her; she just wants to find something to criticize.

Here's the last one. It's poker night and you're sitting around the table with your buddies. The dealer deals, and your friend across the table looks at his cards, pulls at his collar and says, "Does anyone else think it's hot in here?"

Now what's your reaction? Is he bluffing? Does he have a bad poker hand? Is the temperature really hot?

You see, that's the essence of good communication—being able to understand the INTENT behind what someone says, not just the literal words.

Thomas Crane, in his book *The Heart of Coaching* (FTA Press, 2012) says, "Each individual has created a reality—a way of looking at and interpreting life and the world—that is separate and distinct from all others. This reality consists of the total of all of the experiences and conditioning each person absorbed from his or her socialization, the development of the genetic heritage he or she carries from birth, and the choices he or she has made along the way.

"These separate realities act as communication filters. Communication filters distort the clarity of a message the same way a prism or camera filter bends or distorts light. They operate at both the transmission point and the reception point—that is, they affect how you say what you say and how others hear it . . . And as the group becomes larger, the potential for confusion and chaos rises exponentially, as each person's filters distorts group communication in unpredictable ways."

ADVANCED COMMUNICATION APTITUDE

The highest-paid, highest-profile people in any field have learned how to masterfully navigate this complicated web of communication filters. We're calling this quality Advanced Communication Aptitude.

Here are some of the common communication filters that can affect how a message is sent and received. They fall into three primary groups of filters: the mental state, the emotional state, and the current state of the relationship.

Mental State

The mental state refers to our frame of mind during the communication experience. Mental state filters can include assumptions, intentions, hidden agendas, beliefs, and judgments about others and self. So, if you're communicating with someone that you think has a hidden agenda, or you make certain assumptions in the communication, that is a mental state filter. People who have Advanced Communication Aptitude are able to recognize their mental filters and the mental filters of others as they affect the communication experience.

Emotional State

The emotional state refers to feelings or emotions that affect the clarity of communication. When we're in a good mood, we're often more resourceful, easygoing, and open to change. When we're feeling threatened, insecure, self-conscious, or stressed out, we're more likely to feel threatened by change and get caught up in defensiveness or protectiveness in our communications. People who have Advanced Communication Aptitude are able to manage their own emotional states as well as those of others so that they can get their message across and clearly understand the message of others.

Relationship State

The last category of Communication Filters is the current state of the relationship. Did you ever notice how a simple phrase like "that's great" can mean so many different things, depending on the state of the relationship? For example, one employee says to another: "The district manager is coming." The second one says, "That's great." Depending on the state of the relationship between the employee and the district manager, the term "that's great" could be sarcastic and mean something negative, or the term "that's great" could mean that it really is great. And, as anyone who has ever been in a long-term relationship knows, the state of a relationship can change from day to day, sometimes hour to hour!

IMPROVING YOUR APTITUDE FOR COMMUNICATION

OK, now before we get to some tips on how to develop your own Advanced Communication Aptitude, let's talk for a minute about some surprising benefits of good communication skills. This research comes from the bestselling book *Crucial Conversations: Tools for Talking When Stakes Are High* by Kerry Patterson, Joseph Grenny, Ron McMillan, and Al Switzler (McGraw-Hill Education, 2011).

What would you say if we told you that the ability to master important discussions is a key to a healthier and longer life? It's true!

Researchers studied the immune systems of couples who had been married an average of 42 years by comparing those who argued constantly with those who resolved their differences effectively. It turns out that even if you have the same argument for years and years, it's still harmful to your immune system. And, of course, the weaker your immune system, the worse your health is.

Another set of studies looked at how effective communication impacted the survival rate of people with a life-threatening illness. They looked at a group of people who'd contracted malignant skin cancer and taught half of them some specific communication skills. The other half didn't get the training. The groups met six times, and the researchers followed up five years later. The ones who had learned to communicate effectively had a two-thirds decrease in the death rate over the ones who didn't learn the techniques. Can you imagine? Learning to improve your Advanced Communication Aptitude can save your life!

OK, so how CAN you improve your Advanced Communication Aptitude? We've developed the ACA model of communication to better help you understand how those who are in the top 2% of their fields communicate. The term ACA stands for Ask, Consider, and Act.

Ask

The first A stands for Ask. What that means is that you need to listen for the relevant information, taking into account any communication filters that the person might be operating with. Common ways to ask include the phrases:

"What's going on?"

"I'd really like to hear your input on this."

"Please let me know if you see it differently."

"Don't worry about hurting my feelings. I'd really like to know your thoughts."

Then you need to reflect back your understanding of the relevant information.

"OK, so let me make sure I understand . . ."

Now, it's important to make sure that your own filters aren't affecting the communication. These phrases and questions should be said with an attitude of openness. If you feel that emotions are running high, take a break and come back to the conversation when you've evaluated your own filters.

Consider

The next step in the model is Consider. In this model, you want to identify the communication style of the person you are communicating with. Then, using the person's communication style, you share all relevant information, including what you learned from the other person and what you're bringing to the conversation.

Act

Finally, you move to the third stage in the ACA model, which is to Act. This is a critical part of the conversation because a conversation is not the same thing as a decision. If you're not "on the same page," as they say, about what is going to come after the conversation, expectations can be violated later. One person can think the conversation meant one thing, and the other can think it meant something completely different.

The way to prevent this is, before you make a decision about what the next steps are, jointly decide how to decide. Obviously, there are times when it's pretty clear who is making the decision. If your boss or commanding officer says to do something, guess what? You're going to do it. But if there's no clear line of authority, you have to come to a joint decision on how best to make the decision.

According to the authors of *Crucial Conversations*, there are four ways to make a decision. They are: command, consult, vote, and consensus. Command is when one person makes the decision and doesn't really need anyone's input. Consult is when one person makes the decision, but they get the input of others before choosing. Voting is when everyone has a say in the final outcome, but not everyone will agree. Majority rules. And consensus is when everyone must buy into the decision.

So, in the Act stage of the model, you jointly decide how to decide, then make decisions based on one of the four methods above. Either one person in command makes the decision, someone makes the final decision but consults others, all the relevant parties vote and majority rules, or you work to get a consensus.

Once this is done and the decisions have been made, it's important to clarify everyone's roles. You need to decide WHO does WHAT by WHEN, and what it's going to look like when it's done.

ACA IN ACTION

OK, let's take our model for a test drive. Here is a scenario. After a long, tiring business trip, you arrive at your hotel eager to check in and get some rest before an important meeting with a client in the morning. You approach the front desk clerk, a man named Jerry who looks to be about 55 years old. Without looking up, Jerry asks, "Name?"

After providing him with your name, you try and engage him in some small talk about the weather, but he's not responsive. He simply stares at his computer screen typing away. Finally, he states matter-of-factly that he doesn't see a record of your reservation. When you tell him that the reservation was made weeks ago, he asks to see the confirmation number, which you unfortunately left on your desk at home. Jerry gives you a skeptical look leaving you feeling like a kid who just made a bad excuse for why he didn't bring his homework to school.

You're at a standstill. Jerry doesn't seem too eager to want to help you, and you need to get some sleep. How can you use the ACA model to communicate effectively with Jerry?

First, ask some questions to see if you can draw out what his communication filters might be. You might say, "Jerry, what's going on?" "You don't have a reservation in the system." "When this has happened in the past with other customers, what usually happens?" Jerry's answers will tell you a lot about both his filters and what might be a positive solution to the problem. If he says, "Well, the only time this happens is when the customer makes a mistake about the date of the reservations; the computer doesn't make mistakes," then you know that Jerry has an emotional filter of defensiveness. You're going to need to get his guard down by communicating that you don't think it's his fault.

So you ask, "What happens when a customer makes a mistake like that?"

Asking this question gets around his defensiveness filter and lets him know that you're not trying to blame him.

Jerry might then say, "Well sometimes we can see if there's a room in a nearby hotel that's open."

Then you reflect back your understanding of what he just said. "So, sometimes when a customer makes a mistake about their reservations, you can check and see if there's another room available in a nearby hotel?"

Jerry might answer, "I'm not saying there is. I'm just saying that sometimes that's what happens."

Next you move over to the Consider side of the model. You identify their communication style. You identify that they are a left-brained visual person. To communicate with this type, you need to be concise and provide some kind of visual aid to make your point.

You want to share all relevant information, but in this case because you've identified his style as a left-brained visual, you don't want to give him a sob story about how tired you are. Instead, you take out a piece of paper that shows the mapped location of where your meeting is. You say, "OK, Jerry. Here's my situation, and maybe you can help me. I picked this hotel because I have a meeting at 8:30 A.M. tomorrow morning at this address. This seems to be the closest hotel to that address, right? But the computer doesn't show that I have a reservation here. If I were to have to stay somewhere else, is there another hotel that's close to where I'm having my meeting?"

So now you've shared all relevant information in a way that is consistent with his communication style.

Finally, you're moving on to the Act part of the model. Again, you have to jointly decide how to decide. You say, "Jerry, I need a place to stay that's close to my meeting, and I don't seem to have a reservation for here for tonight. Is this something we can solve together?"

Because his communication filters have been cleared up, Jerry is far more likely to collaborate with you on a solution. Jerry is likely to say something like, "Let me call this one hotel that is about a mile away from here and see if they have anything open." You're going to get a lot farther with Jerry using the ACA model of communication than if you get angry and committed to the idea that you did indeed make a reservation for tonight and this particular hotel.

The highest-paid, highest-profile people in every field know that having Advanced Communication Aptitude and using the ACA model of communication in ALL situations is the cornerstone to success. It's not something they turn on and off. They take the time to effectively communicate with every person they deal with.

In our next chapter, we're going to cover the third Rapport quality—being service-oriented.

ENTREPRENEUR FOCUS
Improve Your Communications Skills

Successful leaders are able to meaningfully communicate with others.

Steve Jobs inspired his employees to strive for perfect hardware products. Jack Welch mentored the senior leadership team of GE to new heights. Jeff Bezos is known for articulating the Amazon ethos clearly to employees and the world. All these leaders possess outstanding leadership skills.

Here are 14 ways you can improve your communication skills in order to become a more effective leader.

1. *Learn the basics of nonverbal communication.* One study found that nonverbal communication accounted for 55 percent of how an audience perceived a presenter. That means that the majority of what you say is communicated not through words but through physical cues.

   To communicate clearly and confidently, adopt proper posture. Avoid slouching, folding your arms, or making yourself appear smaller than you are. Instead, fill up the space you are given, maintain eye contact, and (if appropriate) move around the space.

2. *You have to overcommunicate just to communicate.* In 1990, a graduate student at Stanford University was able to prove that presenters overestimate how much listeners understand. In a study that become known as "the tappers and the listeners," one set of participants was asked to tap the melody of 120 famous songs. The other participants were asked to guess what song was being tapped.

   Tappers estimated that 50 percent of the songs tapped would be correctly identified. In reality, only 2.5 percent of the songs were correctly identified. This study shows that it is important to communicate clearly, and to overcommunicate when sharing new ideas. As this study indicates, it is likely that the audience will fail to absorb as much as you expect.

3. *Avoid relying on visual aids.* Steve Jobs instituted a rule at Apple that banned all PowerPoint presentations. Similarly, Sheryl Sandberg instituted a PowerPoint ban at Facebook. Both leaders realized that PowerPoint presentations can hinder rather than help communication.

Be prepared to use words, compelling storytelling, and nonverbal cues to communicate your point with the audience. Avoid using visual aids unless absolutely necessary.

4. *Ask for honest feedback.* As with most leadership skills, receiving honest feedback from peers, managers, and members of your team is critical to becoming a better communicator. If you regularly solicit feedback, others will help you to discover areas for improvement that you might have otherwise overlooked.

5. *Engage the audience in discussion.* Regardless of how compelling the speaker is, all audiences have limited attention spans. To become a more effective communicator, make presentations and discussions interactive. Ask the audience a question, encourage people to call out their thoughts during a brainstorming session, or at the very least ask hypothetical questions to stimulate the audience.

6. *Start and end with key points.* Think back to the "tappers and listeners" study mentioned earlier. Clear communication is paramount. To ensure that the audience understands the key takeaways from a presentation, reiterate key points at the start and finish. This can also be accomplished by providing attendees with a one-pager that includes key points the audience should consider throughout the presentation.

7. *Use the PIP approach.* A common framework used by business experts, like those at McKinsey, is the purpose, importance, preview (PIP) approach to presentation introductions. Following this approach, the speaker first states the purpose of the presentation, and then shares why the presentation is important by reviewing implications and possible outcomes.

Finally, the presenter gives a preview of the topics that will be discussed. This framework is a useful way to get audiences excited about the presentation, helping them to focus on your message and key takeaways.

8. *Record important presentations for posterity.* It can take a good deal of time and energy to communicate effectively. In cases where you may need to give the same presentation multiple times, consider recording it and sharing it in the future.

   Platforms such as Wistia and Zoom allow speakers to record themselves delivering a presentation. These video-recording platforms allow presenters to edit the video to make it more engaging and helpful. They also provide admins with metrics about viewer engagement.

   Recorded presentations can be especially helpful for communicators who need to regularly provide training in a company that is hiring employees quickly.

9. *Master the art of timing.* While some of their jokes might not be appropriate for the workplace, standup comedians are certainly effective communicators. Comedians, including Chris Rock and Dave Chappelle, are able to host compelling 90-minute comedy shows, in part because they have mastered the art of timing.

   Great comedians, like all great communicators, are able to feel out their audience to determine when to move to a new topic or to reiterate an idea.

10. *Get comfortable speaking extemporaneously.* When lawyers present a case in front of the U.S. Supreme Court, they typically speak extemporaneously. That is to say, the lawyers write down a series of topics they intend to discuss, but they do not memorize what they will say word for word. This method of communicating allows the attorneys to cover all the necessary points, while giving them flexibility as to how to communicate based on audience reaction or questions.

   Business communicators should consider adopting an extemporaneous speaking style. It takes practice, but it will allow for more natural communication and can help with audience engagement.

11. *Get to know your audience.* To communicate effectively, it is important to get to know your audience first. Each audience is unique and will have different preferences and cultural norms that should be considered when communicating. A good way to understand expectations is to ask members of the audience for examples of good communicators within the organization.

12. *Add novelty to improve audience retention.* A recent study revealed that people generally retain more information when presented with novel, as opposed to routine, situations. To help audience members retain information, consider injecting some sort of novel event into a presentation. This might be something funny or that simply catches people by surprise.

13. *Focus on earning respect instead of laughs.* It can be tempting to communicate with others a lightheartedly; after all, this can be a good way to make friends in a professional setting. But remember that the most successful communicators are those who have earned respect, rather than laughs. While telling a joke or two to warm up an audience can be effective, avoid ending a presentation with a laugh.

14. *Be a listener.* "Listen more than you talk." This is what Richard Branson tells businesspeople who want to connect with others. To communicate effectively, first listen to what others have to say. Then you can provide a thoughtful answer that shows you have taken those ideas into account.

Communicating clearly is one of the most effective skills you can cultivate as a business leader. Remember to communicate using nonverbal and verbal cues. Listen carefully to what others have to say, and overcommunicate in novel ways to ensure the content of the conversation sticks with the audience.

12

THE SERVICE PARADOX

In this chapter, we'll cover the third quality in our Rapport category—being service-oriented.

In *Lead the Field*, Earl Nightingale describes the importance of being service-oriented this way. He says:

> Working hard is not enough. Your rewards in life will always match the level of your service. Input determines output. Seek to serve. You must not only work hard but smart. Many people are ignorant of the principal law of cause and effect. For every action there is an equal and opposite reaction. Our rewards in life will always match our service. "As you sow, so shall you also reap." If anyone is dissatisfied with his rewards, he needs to examine his service.

Each of serves a portion of humanity, all those with whom you come in contact. We serve others. Others serve us.

We need each other. Every time we use a product or service, someone is serving us. Rewards are of the tangible type but also intangible, such as happiness and peace of mind. Whatever it is you seek in the form of rewards, you must first earn in the form of service. The wood must be put in before you can get warmth. You cannot get maximum heat with too small a supply of wood. Think not about future rewards but about present service.

Discontent is measured by the distance between what you want and what you have. Constructive discontent results in an upward spiral. Determine what you want. Measure the distance between you and your goal and determine ways of increasing your service. People will be happy to supply you with the living you need if you'll think of some way to serve them. Never seek to be given anything. Seek to serve in such a way that you'll be rewarded. Start where you are. Our job is to do the sowing, the rest will take care of itself.

You can always tell what people have done by observing what they have. You can measure their contribution to society by societies contribution to them. My rewards in life will be in exact proportion to my service. "How can I increase my service today?" We must work intelligently, seeking ways to increase our service and thereby increasing our rewards. Do it now!

Earl perfectly describes what we are calling the service paradox. The more you serve others, the more you receive in return. And the more you receive, the more resources you have to share with others. The people who are the highest-paid, highest-profile people in any industry got that way because they understand the truth in what Earl Nightingale said. My rewards in life will be in exact proportion to my service.

THE SIX PRINCIPLES

Let's walk through the six principles to the service paradox.

Principle #1
The person you serve may not always appreciate it or may come to take it for granted. But a reward will come to you from another source.

Here's an example of that. A man named Bob was working in his office one day and noticed that one of his co-workers was having a rough day. So, on his lunch break, he bought her a large container of animal crackers to cheer her up. She was thrilled! But a few weeks later, the co-worker came to Bob and said, "Bob, we ran out of crackers. We love them so much. Could you get some more?" He didn't want to do it. He told her, "It's different when I do it because I want to, but now you are trying to make me go get them. It's not the same." But she kept standing there. So Bob agreed to do it.

On his lunch break, Bob drove five miles to the store and had to park at the very end of a large parking lot. It was bitter cold—in the single digits. But when he got out of his car, he stepped into summer. How? Seagulls. There were seagulls flying in the parking lot of this store in the dead of winter! Bob closed his eyes and was suddenly transported back in time to a memory of feeding seagulls on the beach. When he went into the store, along with the animal crackers, Bob bought a loaf of bread. He spent ten minutes feeding the seagulls in the freezing cold, laughing as they crashed and dive-bombed to get the bread. He became so overpowered by the sheer number of seagulls that he finally had to dump the loaf of bread and run laughing to the safety of his car. In doing a favor for his co-worker, Bob was treated to a mini-vacation in the middle of winter and was reminded of better days ahead.

Principle #2
You have to seize the moments to serve when they happen, even if you're afraid.

Actress and comedienne Rosie O'Donnell tells a story about her son, who was 6 years old at the time of the September 11th attacks in New York. Shortly after the attacks, Rosie's son Parker insisted that she take him to a fire station, even though she feared he was too young to deal with all the pain there. But he said, "Mommy, I need to go." Eventually she took him there, and there were these shell-shocked firemen dressed in their formal blue uniforms on the way to yet another funeral and grieving for 15 of their firehouse brothers who'd died in the attacks on the World Trade Center. Parker walked over to a very big fireman and tugged on his coat. The fireman stooped down and Parker said, "I'm sorry your friends died to save us. But they're with God now." And Parker started to cry. And the fireman started to cry. And then Rosie started to cry, and everyone who had heard started to cry. Rosie realized that while she had been wanting to protect her son, thinking it would be too much for him, he ended up serving them all in a way that none of them would ever forget.

Principle #3
Your reward doesn't always come in the way you expect.

Here is an example. Once, a friend of mine was honest when the cashier at her market gave her too much change. Well, the next week, she ran into the same market for some milk. Sitting at the register were a stack of coupons worth $13. And these were coupons for cash off . . . they weren't dependent on her needing to buy certain items. She was able to use them the next time she went to the market to do her regular, weekly shopping and deduct $13 from her bill. So, for my friend, the service that she provided by being honest and saving the market money they would have lost was rewarded to her in the form of coupons that saved her actual cash.

Principle #4
Serving and receiving are halves of a circle.

While in a giving state of mind, you have to be open to receiving, too. As in the story with Bob and the seagulls, Bob was able to see that the experience of feeding the gulls was a positive reward for his service to his co-worker because his mind was open to it. He wasn't grumbling about having to go to the store and racing in to get the crackers and be done with it. He was open and in the moment so that he could receive the reward. My friend with the cash machine was able to make the connection between the coupons she found and her honesty the week earlier. In order to fully receive the rewards that come to you, you need to keep your mind open to what you are receiving while you are serving. The more you focus on the little ways that you are blessed and are receiving, the more you will receive. It's circular.

Principle #5
You may never know the impact of your service.

U.S. Senator and former presidential candidate John McCain tells a story about a gift he received from a fellow prisoner when he was a prisoner of war in Vietnam. Senator McCain was imprisoned for five and a half years, and much of that time was spent in solitary confinement. He recalls that Christmas was the most difficult time of the year for him. As he tells in the book, *The Right Words at the Right Time* (Atria Books, 2004), by Marlo Thomas, one of his fellow prisoners, Ernie, tapped a message on their shared wall (an act that was strictly forbidden) on Christmas Eve. The message was simply to convey their shared hope that they would be home for Christmas the following year. McCain writes, "That simple message, in my darkest hour, strengthened my will to live."

You see, Ernie didn't know whether or not McCain could hear the tapping. He had no idea that it was the darkest hour of his life. But the gift he gave, not knowing whether it was even heard, is what helped McCain survive solitary confinement and return to a life of service in the U.S. government.

Principle #6
Your service may be a small contribution, but it matters to someone.

In 2009, President Barack Obama gave a speech designed to inspire Americans to service. In the speech, he shared a well-known story by anthropologist Loren Eiseley about a little boy on the beach. It goes like this.

An old man walking along the beach at dawn sees a young man picking up starfish and throwing them out to sea. "Why are you doing that?" the old man inquired. The young man explained that the starfish had been stranded on the beach by a receding tide and would soon die in the daytime sun. "But the beach goes on for miles," the old man said. "And there are so many! How can your effort make any difference?" The young man looked at the starfish in his hand and without hesitating threw it to safety in the sea. He looked up at the old man, smiled and said, "It will make a difference to that one."

You may have heard that story before. But what you may NOT know is that it actually became true. Later that year in the UK, a storm threw more than 10,000 starfish on the beach after the sea had washed them from their feeding grounds. Margaret Perrot, a 63-year-old woman, was distraught after seeing them on her morning walk. Like the little boy in the story, she walked along the beach looking for starfish that were still alive and then returned them to sea. Sadly, most of the starfish perished on the beach that day. But her actions made a difference to the few she saved.

We are all connected, and when we serve, we receive.

INTEGRATING SERVICE INTO YOUR DAILY LIFE

So how can you integrate these ideas into your daily life? Let's look at how some of the highest-paid, highest-profile people have done it.

There's a program called Famous Fone Friends, where celebrities, such as Bryan Cranston, Reba McIntire, Henry Winkler, and dozens of others, make telephone calls to seriously ill children throughout the U.S. and Canada. While you may not be a celebrity, you can certainly bring cheer to ill children at your local children's hospital.

Athletes such as John Elway, Dan Marino, Jerry Rice, and Michael Jordan often play in celebrity golf tournaments. While you might not be able to play alongside these high-profile athletes, you can certainly volunteer for a charity sporting event. Even if you don't play a sport, most events need other services like security, setup and clean-up, or some other kind of help.

Former U.S. President Jimmy Carter has almost become more famous for his humanitarian work than for anything he did as president. He is a key figure in the Habitat for Humanity project, which builds homes for those in need. You could certainly volunteer for a Habitat for Humanity near you. Or you could serve food at a homeless shelter, or donate items from your garage to charity.

Actress Sandra Bullock donated $1 million to earthquake relief in Haiti in 2010. Madonna gave $250,000. You may not be able to give such huge quantities of money to disaster relief, but you can give a dollar. You can give coins to the Salvation Army outside the store during the holidays.

You see? No matter who you are or how much or little you have to give, being service-oriented is about having an attitude of service and giving on a daily basis. It's not always about donating to something big. Sometimes it's just picking up a piece of trash you see lying on the ground, even if you didn't put it there. It's buying a sandwich for a guy you see eating out of the trash. It's what you do EVERY DAY.

FOCUS ON MORE THAN YOUR FEELINGS

There's one final thing about the service paradox that's important to mention. Some people engage in service activities because it makes them feel good about themselves. They volunteer to clean trash off the beach or something and then go back to their lives, thinking mainly of their own needs and desires. For them, service is an activity that is more self-oriented. It's done so that the person can have a sense of themselves as a "good person." And while any service is better than no service, that's different than what we're talking about here. Because another paradox in the service paradox is that, very often, serving others doesn't make you feel good when you're doing it. A writer friend of mine served breakfast at a homeless shelter the other day. As she looked into the eyes and saw the gratitude of the people she was feeding, she didn't feel good. She felt terrible. She felt overwhelmed at the magnitude of the problem of hunger in our world today. What good is feeding one person when they're just going to be hungry again tomorrow, she wondered?

But as she was driving home, sad and frustrated, she realized that this is the very reason why she wants to be in the top 2% of her field. Because when you're one of the highest-paid, highest-profile people in your industry, you can effect a bigger change. You'll have more visibility to change the things in this world that matter to you. You'll have the money and resources to make a much bigger impact.

The service paradox, really, is that serving others doesn't necessarily make you feel good. And you might not see how your actions can make a difference. But, as William Penn, the founder of the province that later became the state of Pennsylvania said, "He that does good for good's sake seeks neither paradise nor reward, but he is sure of both in the end."

In our next chapter, we're going to cover the fourth Rapport quality—having fulfilling relationships.

ENTREPRENEUR FOCUS
Develop Your Servant Leadership Mindset

Like pretty much everything nowadays, the concept of leadership has morphed and evolved into something our parents or grandparents would not recognize. A few decades ago, things seemed simpler. Being the boss automatically made you a leader in the eyes of employees. Now, everyone wears more than one hat, lines are more blurred, and being a boss doesn't automatically make you a leader. Leadership is no longer concentrated at the top. It has trickled down the organizational chart.

With all the tools we have today, there's no excuse *not* to be a better leader. We'll go a step further and say that being a good leader isn't even enough. You have to be a servant leader. Servant leadership is defined as a "philosophy and set of practices that enriches the lives of individuals, builds better organizations, and ultimately creates a more just and caring world."

In 2018, Jeffrey Hayzlett wrote the book, *The Hero Factor: How Great Leaders Transform Organizations and Create a Winning Culture* (Entrepreneur Press). In it, he talked about finding mentors to guide you throughout your journey. To become a hero leader, you must seek the advice of those who have come before you—those who have been there and done that and have the battle scars to prove it. Hero leaders surround themselves with mentors and experts who are keen on opportunities that benefit them (and others), who have a finger on the pulse and know the answers for problems that may be plaguing their industry.

That is what servant leadership is. It's not about being an errand boy or bowing down to your superiors. It's about leading by example and paying it forward. Being a servant leader is not just about what you can do for others outside the organization. It is being a servant to your values, creating a culture that reflects those same values and embraces diversity, including diversity of thought, as well as a willingness to learn the courage of your convictions.

What are your company's values? Is everyone on the team clear on what the company, and you as a leader, stand for? According to Gallup data, only 27 percent of employees strongly believe in their company's values. If we are to be successful leaders, those numbers have to go *way* up. How can that be done? Here are four steps to develop into a better servant leader.

1. Encourage Diversity of Thought

Diversity encompasses myriad traits. It's about more than just gender, race, ethnicity, sexuality, or political and religious beliefs. It's about thinking different, too. Having a diverse team fosters an environment that people want to be a part of. According to research by Glassdoor, 67 percent of active job seekers said a diverse workplace is important to them when considering job offers, and 57 percent of employers want to make a bigger effort to prioritize diversity.

Servant leadership encourages everyone to think outside the box and considers every perspective when tasked with moving the needle forward. The final decision is the by-product of a collective collaboration and exchange of ideas. Power never rests with one person, but with everyone on the team contributing to the end result. Are you giving everyone a seat at the table? Why the heck not?

2. Create a Culture of Trust

Trust is one of the hardest things to regain once it's broken. How can any leader create a culture of trust? By clearly communicating to everyone in the company what the mission is, what values they are expected to live by are, and what the overall vision is. A global database by Gallup reveals that just one in three employees strongly agree that they trust the leadership in their organization.

How can executives build a higher level of trust? By being crystal clear about everything. All communications need to be specific and disseminated to every single level of the organization, top to bottom. If you are not transparent and fail to lead with a clear purpose, no one is going to follow you. Being transparent foments trust, which has a direct correlation to work performance. Remember, trust is earned, not given. Have you earned your team's trust?

3. Have an Unselfish Mindset

It's not about you. It never was, and it never will be. It's about the people who make it all work. Ask yourself: Where would you be without the cogs that make the engine run? One common mistake leaders make is thinking that profits and people are to be seen as separate entities, when they should go hand-in-hand. You can't have one without the other, so why keep them separate? Great hero leaders help facilitate the success of others and make everyone feel valued and that their contributions matter to the overall success of the company. According to Survey Monkey, 43 percent of respondents said that feeling appreciated makes them more confident. More so, 78 percent felt happy after receiving gratitude.

Great leaders drive change in many ways, but unselfishness is what ultimately allows them to scale their businesses and create a long-lasting legacy.

4. Foster Leadership in Others

Leaders who understand the power of building a great team understand the need to develop the next generation of leaders. It is more than just mentoring someone in your midst who has the potential to take your job one day. With baby boomers retiring, it is crucial that leaders mold the next generation, but they have a tough assignment ahead. A white paper about HR and millennials states that 63 percent of millennials feel a lack of leadership development. This should frighten us, because who will be left to take over the businesses when we're enjoying retirement? If we don't shape up, the answer will be *no one*!

Fostering leadership comes in many forms, including coaching, mentorship, and growth. Take the time to teach someone the ropes, to offer words of encouragement, and answer questions these young leaders have for you. Great leaders give back. Great leaders are able to put together a diverse group of people from all walks of life. In fact, diverse organizations are 1.7 times more likely to develop innovative leaders.

Servant leaders give more of themselves not because they have to, but because they want to. Servant leaders are transparent, honest, and yes, even vulnerable. That sounds like it would be a weakness, but it can help build you up as a leader and let others see you as a human being, not just the person who signs the checks.

13

THE ART OF SELECTIVE ENGAGEMENT

W e are on the fourth of the Rapport qualities that we've identified as being present in the highest-paid, highest-profile people in any industry. In this chapter, we'll cover the idea that the top 2% have fulfilling relationships.

The key to having fulfilling relationships is intent. You have to DECIDE that you'll have fulfilling relationships and then engage with the people in your life in ways that will allow the relationship to be fulfilling to you. And this doesn't go only for romantic or family relationships. We're talking about ALL your relationships, from the very intimate to relationships with strangers.

We've titled this chapter "The Art of Selective Engagement" because it captures the essence of what the most successful STARS know. You have to be selective in how you engage with the people you're in a relationship with. You need to treat your spouse differently than you treat your children. You need to engage differently with your sister than you do your co-workers. You even need to intentionally select how you engage with members of the public. This chapter is going to cover the idea of selective engagement with all the different types of relationships you have.

VISUALIZE YOUR RELATIONSHIP CIRCLE

Think about a diagram that represents the various relationships you might have in your life. It looks largely like a dart board. It's a circle, and within the circle are several smaller circles. The outer circle represents the people in the public who you don't really know. You just interact with them as you go out in the world. The next circle in represents your functional friends. These are people you might socialize with, like co-workers or members of a church group. They could be your kids' friends' parents or members of your reading club. You're friendly with them, but you wouldn't call them at 2 A.M. with a problem. Next we have the circle that represents your family relationships. Of course, you can put your family wherever on the diagram you want. But the inner circle contains your children, your siblings, and your parents. Again, don't write me an email and tell me your crazy brother should be further out on the circle. You can put him wherever you want. This is for illustration purposes only. The next smallest circle contains your true friends. These ARE the people you can call at 2 A.M. with a problem. The second to smallest circle is your spouse or significant other. This is your intimate relationship—the person with whom you can share just about anything. If you aren't married or in a relationship, sometimes a best friend can be this close. And the smallest, inner circle represents your relationship with yourself and your source of spiritual inspiration. Your spiritual center is the point that is at the center of this diagram.

Engaging with the Public

Let's work from the outside of the diagram in and talk about selective engagement with the public. How do you present yourself in public?

When Earl Nightingale recorded *Lead the Field*, this wasn't even an issue. People didn't wear their pajamas to the market. You didn't overhear heated personal arguments via cell phones. It was a different time, and it wasn't as important to consciously select how you're going to engage with the public.

But nowadays, you must. The truth is, almost everyone has a camera with them at all times in the form of a cell phone. Even if you don't have to worry about paparazzi, you can still be caught standing next to someone doing something, and the next thing you know, you're on YouTube. Do you really want to be all over the internet wearing your SpongeBob SquarePants pajamas? This doesn't mean you need to go business casual for a run to the convenience store, but if you're going to be one of the highest-profile people in your industry, it's a good idea to think about how you're presenting yourself when you go out in public.

A modern offshoot of this idea is how you present yourself in social media. We live in an interconnected internet world, and the things you post on Facebook, Twitter, or YouTube are likely to be seen by complete strangers. Celebrities and other notable individuals have been fired when they posted controversial comments on Twitter. It's a good idea to be consciously aware of how you are presenting yourself on the internet. Leave the off-color cartoons and jokes to those in the OTHER 98%.

Another, related topic has to do with how you treat others when in public. Do you cut in front of others in line? Are you rude to waiters and cashiers? Do you demonstrate road rage? Of course, YOU don't do these things, but you probably know people who do. What does that do to your opinion of them? Every person you meet should be considered a potential customer. Here's an example.

A young man was considering going into acting, so he became an extra on a movie set. This was in the 1960s and was a movie that had a lot of extras. This young actor was thrilled to be working alongside one of the most beloved actors of his time. The young man, however, decided not to become an actor and went on to have a successful business in a small town. Many years later, the young man, who was no longer a young man, attended a party that the famous actor was also attending. Being social, the man walked up to the famous actor and said, "It's great to see you again! You probably don't remember, but we worked together several years ago on a movie set." "Really? We worked together?" "Yes. It was in THIS movie" and he said the name of the movie. The actor looked the man up and down in shock. "You were in that movie with me? What on earth HAPPENED to you? I mean, look at me! I went on to become famous and successful! And you moved HERE?"

Not only did the man hear the actor insult him, but everyone else at the party did, too. The actor remained one of America's most beloved figures until the time of his death. But those who were there always remembered the actor differently after that day.

Even if you don't plan to be famous, you still need to be selective about what you say or do in public. You wouldn't see Diane Sawyer going to the market in her sweats. I can't imagine the Supreme Court Justices uploading a YouTube video of their Christmas office party. This program is designed to help you become one of the highest-paid highest PROFILE people in your field. Whether you have a public forum like a TV or radio show, or are just going to the market for a few items, behave like you're in the top 2% of your field.

Engaging with Functional Friends

Next come your functional friends. These are people you might call friends, but if you changed jobs or moved away, the friendship would probably fade away. How can the art of selective engagement help you create fulfilling relationships with this group?

In order to consciously select how to engage with functional friends, you need to define the boundaries of the relationship. You have to select what information is relevant to share and what's too personal. And you have to know what to do if the other person doesn't understand those boundaries!

Here is an example. A friend of mine, we'll call her Tammy, used to be a Girl Scout Troop leader. This is a great example of functional friendship. The adults get together with their daughters, but it's for a specific function. Well, one year, Tammy's troop got a new family, and it was a single mom who was going through a nasty divorce. Every week before the meeting, this woman would tell Tammy all the personal details of the divorce—her husband's affair, how much the lawyer was costing, et cetera. That's not selective engagement. My friend just stood there thinking, "I do NOT want to know all this stuff!"

Those who are the highest-profile people in any industry are discerning about what personal information they share. Sometimes functional friends can feel like real friends, but the STARS realize that there is a difference. Be selective about what information you share.

What about gossip? This is the circle on our model where gossip occurs. Of course, YOU wouldn't talk about someone who isn't there. But how can you gracefully get out of situations where gossiping is going on? Here are three suggestions for avoiding gossip.

TIP #1: See the Birdy

When someone begins gossiping to you, redirect the conversation to something else. Doing this gracefully can take some practice, but you can take something that the other person said and use that as a launching pad for something else. "Speaking of Bob, I heard that we're all getting new software updates." If that doesn't work, move on to Tip #2.

TIP #2: "Back Atcha"

To do this, turn the conversation back to the gossiper and start asking about his or her life. It has been said that a gossip is one who talks to you about others; a bore is one who talks to you about herself; and a brilliant conversationalist is one who talks to you about yourself.

TIP #3: Say What You Need to Say

Sometimes the only way to get out of a gossiping situation is to be direct about it. You can say something like, "Look guys, I'm not comfortable with this conversation. Can we talk about something else?"

The main thing to remember when developing fulfilling relationships with functional friends is to understand the boundaries and limitations of the relationship. As football coach Lou Holtz put it, "Don't tell your problems to people. 80% don't care, and the other 20% are glad you have them."

Engaging with Family

In the next circle toward the center is your family. The reason that we put children in the same circle as other family members is because, while parenting is one of the more rewarding relationships a person can have, it's not necessarily one that is filled with positive emotions most of the time. In an article in *The New York Times*, researcher Martin Seligman says, "If we just wanted positive emotions, our species would have died out a long time ago," he says. "We have children to pursue other elements of well-being. We want meaning in life. We want relationships." In another quote, he says, "Paradoxically, your happiness is raised by the very fact that you are willing to have your happiness lowered through years of dirty diapers, tantrums and back-talk. Willingness to accept unhappiness from children is a source of happiness."

The same thing goes for your other family members. Siblings and parents (as well as stepparents) can provide us with support, but they can also hurt us the most. How can we practice the Art of Selective Engagement with family members?

Again, the key lies in understanding the individuals in the relationship. If you know your mother doesn't approve of that tattoo you got last summer, cover it up when you're around her. If your sister is always bragging about how great her life is, let her be that way. You see, the key in dealing with family is to accept their love and support in the way that they CHOOSE to give it, rather than in the way you want to receive it. If you're focusing on how they DO show their love, then you'll be fulfilled in the relationship. If you're expecting people to behave differently, you'll be frustrated.

Before we get on to the next circle, let's talk for a bit about forgiveness. One's family is usually the place where the most hurt occurs. Few people make it to adulthood without needing to come to terms with something that someone in the family has done to them.

Again, thinking of The Art of Selective Engagement, you have the power to create the relationships with the people in your life. You can choose to have relationships with those who support and fulfill you, and you can pull back and be more selective with those who don't.

Engaging with True Friends

The next circle in is where your true friends are. You'll notice that we put your friends in a closer circle than family. If you're so close to your daughter or your sister that you consider them a friend, they can go in this circle.

How can you apply The Art of Selective Engagement in friendship? Here are three ways.

1. *Make time for your friendship.* In this day and age, it's too easy to let life get in the way of friendship. We find ourselves spending more time with our functional friends than our true friends. Instead, select time to be with your true friends—even if it's over the phone, by text, or online.
2. *Support your friend's choices.* Sure, there are times when you can say "I told you so." Don't. Only engage your friend in ways that support or uplift him or her. A friend is someone who understands your past, believes in your future, and accepts you just the way you are.
3. *Don't be afraid of the difficult conversations.* A true friend isn't afraid of saying the truth. But understand the right time for honesty. There is a time for silence. A time to let go and allow people to make mistakes on their life path. And a time to prepare to pick up the pieces when it's all over.

The Art of Selective Engagement in friendship can be summed up by Ralph Waldo Emerson, "The only way to have a friend is to be one."

Engaging with Your Significant Other

OK, now let's move on to the circle with your spouse or significant other. How can you practice The Art of Selective Engagement in your romantic relationship?

For every action or statement in a relationship, there are two ways to take it. You can assume a loving intent or a hurtful intent. If you choose to assume a loving intent, and respond in kind with love, your relationship will be fulfilling.

Here are four principles to apply The Art of Selective Engagement in your romantic relationship:

1. *Talk about problems when they arise.* Don't let them build up, because if you're angry about one thing it will spill over into other areas.

2. *Select the right time to discuss issues in the relationship.* Set aside a specific time to talk about both positive and negative things in the relationship. If you're trying to share something wonderful while your spouse is checking emails, he or she isn't likely to be as engaged as if you'd chosen a better time.

3. *Practice loving acceptance.* You didn't fall in love with your-self. Your partner is different than you are and has strengths and shortcomings. If you selectively focus on your partner's strengths, they will grow. This melts defensiveness and moti-vates partners to want to please each other.

4. *Give your mate the benefit of the doubt.* There are usually two ways you can react to something. Whenever you're hurt, angry, or disappointed, step aside and see if there's an explanation that can allow you to see your partner in a loving light.

The Art of Selective Engagement in a romantic relationship is about choosing to always see that person you fell in love with.

Engaging with Yourself

Finally, we come to the innermost circle—the one that contains only you and your source of spiritual inspiration. What does The Art of Selective Engagement look like with yourself? It has to do with letting go of your past mistakes.

So, The Art of Selective Engagement when it comes to your relationship with yourself is to see yourself as being connected to your source of spiritual inspiration. For Christians, this would mean seeing yourself as a reflection of God. Buddhists or Hindus say mantras or meditate to stay connected with the Divine. Jews have a special prayer shawl called a Tallit that helps them feel close to their spiritual source. You selectively engage with yourself as a reflection of a Divine being.

French philosopher Pierre Teilhard de Chardin said it best: "We are not human beings having a spiritual experience. We are spiritual beings immersed in a human experience."

Our relationships with others have the ability to complete and fulfill us in a way that nothing else can. The key to having fulfilling relationships is the idea of deciding to do so and selecting to engage with people in a way that allows the relationship to be fulfilling. In our next chapter, we're going to cover the final Rapport quality—the ability to negotiate great deals.

ENTREPRENEUR FOCUS
Building Real Relationships

Some people make it look so effortless and easy when they engage in a new conversation. The best networkers have mastered the law of attraction. They are likable, helpful, emotionally intelligent, and thoughtful.

The successful people you seek to network with likely have well-documented achievement in business and life experience. The leaders you meet who can help you most may easily pick up on when someone is enamored by the financial returns of their success. These same people will feel your authenticity when you engage them with genuine passion. Building a precious new relationship with someone that has an abundance mentality is a process. Remember, it will not happen from one meeting alone.

Following these eight strategies will help you become a more effective networker and build stronger relationships with people of influence and affluence.

You Only Get One First Impression

Energy is the most powerful force on earth. Remind yourself that you are an energy magnet and everyone will be attracted to you. Then, smile and practice it. Expect that people will like you and want to be your friend.

Giving your best introduction, and one that will make you stand out, will not happen automatically. Building relationships starts with thoughtful communication. People judge you and draw initial conclusions about who you are within seconds of meeting you. You only have one chance to make a memorable first impression. What you are in terms of job title and degrees is not as important to someone as your character and who you are.

Deliver a Relevant Message

Communicating a relevant message is important. To do so, you must be aware of who you are talking to, what subjects you are speaking about, and, of course, why should someone listen. Research your audience, relevant news, and current events before attending. Invest your personal time to come prepared with talking points and appropriate questions. Consider connecting with attendees, conference organizers, and even keynote speakers on LinkedIn with a custom message saying you are looking forward to seeing them at the event. This proactive approach will signal that you are interested and serious about their time and yours.

Be Present

It's the era of smartphones and stupid people. Isn't it ironic that technology brings us closer to people far away but takes us away from people sitting next to us? People feel welcome when they are heard and listened to. Being present in the moment is key to earning trust and respect, which is a precursor to building relationships.

Use Social Media Effectively

How frequently do you check your Facebook, Instagram, LinkedIn, Twitter, or Snapchat on your phone? Networking and building relationships are functions of both in-person and digital interaction.

Social media platforms revolutionize how we communicate and accelerate our access to information. People may be too busy to return a phone call, but they are consistently present on social media. As such, having a representative presence is important.

Today, we can access almost anyone from a device that fits in the palm of our hand. Create a positive internet reputation for yourself and ensure you are well-represented online.

Learn to Listen, and Listen to Learn

When we speak, we share what we already know. When we listen, we learn. Being a good listener is not optional; it is required to build new relationships. When meeting and communicating with new people, we often unintentionally interrupt or cut off someone we just met. Introverts have a competitive advantage because they use their ears and mouth proportionately. People derive happiness and satisfaction from talking about their ideas, knowledge, and experience.

Prepare to Facilitate Conversations

We have all witnessed the awkward silence when meeting someone new. It may have been so uncomfortable that we just walked away from the conversation. This is a lost opportunity to build relationships. Be the catalyst for stimulating conversations and keeping them going with open-ended questions.

Quality over Quantity

Effective networking is the first step to building relationships. There is such pressure associated with going to an event where we are supposed to meet new people. We often hurry to meet and greet as many new faces as we can. There is even a positive aura and feeling of success when we collect and distribute a serious stack of business cards. Always prefer quality over quantity.

Always Follow Up

Most of us have brought home business cards and left them on our desks with the best of intentions. After a week, we remind ourselves we need to follow up. After a month, we may avoid thinking or even looking at them. One month later, we throw them away after sending a generic LinkedIn connection request. Building relationships through networking takes 100 percent effort. Meeting someone requires, at most, 5 percent effort; following up is the other 95 percent. If you tell someone you are going to email or call them, do it. Be patient when following up with new connections.

To win friends and influence people, we need to earn the trust and respect of others. Networking is about giving, not getting. I have found that one of the most effective ways to earn trust is to first gain clarity on what is a qualified and helpful introduction for a new friend.

14

COLLABORATIVE PERSUASION

We are on the fifth and final Rapport quality that we've identified as being present in the highest-paid, highest-profile people in any industry, and that's the ability to negotiate and make great deals.

Let me share with you a story that illustrates the power of negotiation in a setting that most of us are familiar with—buying a used car.

Dave is a 21-year-old college student from California. He doesn't come from a rich family by any means, and so for his birthday, his parents give him the minivan that was in the family for the past ten years. They tell him, "Dave, you can drive the van, fix it up, or trade it in for something else if you want. It's your car to do with what you please."

There's no way Dave is going to drive around college in his mother's old minivan. So he takes the $5,000 that he earned working through high school and the first part of college and decides to trade in the van for a nicer used car. He does his research and identifies a great little convertible that he can pay cash for and he heads on down to the used car dealer with $5,000 cash and the title to the van.

He walks in, and he's the only customer in the place. A salesperson comes over. "Hi, I'm Joe. Can I help you with something?" Now, remember. Dave is a 21-year-old college kid. Joe isn't expecting him to be an excellent negotiator. "Yeah, I'm here to look at that convertible you have over there."

Dave and Joe go for a test drive, and Dave acts the part of a typical college kid, talking about the weather and his weekend plans. But meanwhile, he's mentally checking out the car for points to use in the negotiation later on. He's also getting a feel for Joe and his communication style. He asks, "So, how long has the car been here?" Joe says, "Oh, a few weeks."

They get back to the dealer and Joe says, "OK, the price is $5,990, and with tax and all the fees it comes to $6,750. Did you want to trade in your car?"

"Maybe." Let the negotiating begin.

"OK, so we'll offer you $950 for the van. That brings it down to $5,800. Will that work for you?"

"Well, Joe, the hood is going to need to be repainted because of that oxidation. How about I give you $5,500 and the trade and drive away?"

"Oh man. I don't know. Let me talk to my manager."

Dave waits for what seems like an eternity. Meanwhile now that he knows the condition of the vehicle and what they're asking for it, he sneaks into the restroom and uses his smartphone to run the *Kelly Blue Book* value on the car. It's listed at $6,850.

Joe comes back and says that they have a deal. They're filling out the paperwork when, all of a sudden, the manager comes out and is like, "Oh, there is one thing we forgot to tell you about the car. It's got a crack in the dashboard."

Dave remembers that there was a dash cover on the dashboard but didn't think to look under it. He says, "I need to see it."

The crack is huge, but Dave sees that it's a negotiation point. "Guys, there's no way I can do this. This is a deal-breaker. I appreciate the fact that you were honest about this before I bought the car, but I can't pay $5,500 for a car with a giant crack in the dashboard."

"You can keep the cover on," they say.

"Joe, I can't just keep the cover on. The car has a huge crack! It has to be fixed. I'm sorry."

So, Dave goes to gather his things and pretends to check his emails on his phone to give them time to think of a counteroffer.

Joe comes back and says, "What if we lowered the price $300? This would mean that I'm not getting any profit on the car, but I'm willing to do that."

(Are you recognizing every trick in the book? Waiting until Dave is emotionally committed to buying before they "remember" the crack? Saying that they'll give up their profit? Making him wait?)

"Joe, I appreciate your offer, but I need to think about it. I have no idea what it would even cost to fix such a thing. I'm going to go next door to McDonalds and think it over."

Dave goes to the McDonalds next door and starts calling other car dealers about the repair. One of them tells him, "Well the labor alone would cost $500. I don't know about the part."

Dave searches the internet on his phone and finds the part, and it's about $250. So, he adds on a hundred to that for the negotiation figure and walks back to the dealer.

"OK, here's my suggestion. You can fix the car, and I'll pay $5,500 for it. Or you drop the price to $4,650."

"Oh man, I really can't do that."

"I understand, Joe. It was nice almost doing business with you. I really appreciate your integrity in disclosing the issue to me. I'm sure you'll be able to find another cash buyer who won't mind a giant crack in the dashboard." Dave starts to leave again.

"Wait. Let me see what I can do."

Dave sits down and a full 20 minutes later, Joe comes back. "How about $4,750. Plus, your trade in."

"Deal."

Using the negotiation skills that you're going to learn in this chapter, Dave managed to get the price of the car down from $6,750 to $4,750. That's quite a savings! And it really was a win/win. Dave got the car he wanted for a price he could afford. And Joe was able to sell a car that had been sitting on the lot for a while because it had some minor damage.

COLLABORATIVE PERSUASION

We've titled this chapter "Collaborative Persuasion" because the people who are in the top 2% are the ones who know how to negotiate ETHICALLY. It's not about cheating someone or getting your way at all costs. Sure, there are people who are like that and who achieve some measure of success. But the ones that make it to the top 2% and STAY there, are the ones who know how to collaborate and negotiate ethically. Billionaire J. Paul Getty is quoted as saying, "My father said: 'You must never try to make all the money that's in a deal. Let the other fellow make some money, too, because if you have a reputation for always making all the money, you won't have many deals."

So, what are the steps in Collaborative Persuasion? There are four of them.

1. Understanding the other person's viewpoint
2. Communicating your viewpoint
3. Separating the positions from the problem
4. Jointly creating solutions

Let's go through them.

Step 1: Understanding the Other Person's Viewpoint

Now this step and the next one are closely related to the ACA model of communication that we covered in a previous chapter. So if you haven't read that chapter yet, be sure and do so. A key point in understanding the other person's viewpoint is the idea that their thinking and the filters they have are the source of the differences between the two of you. *The magnitude of any problem has to do with the difference between their viewpoints and yours.* When two people, or groups for that matter, have a conflict, they may be blaming the other person (or group) for something that happened. Most people think that you need to get at the objective truth of what happened. They do research and find facts and data to support their own viewpoints. But ultimately, conflict lies not in objective reality, but in people's minds. Discovering the facts may not solve the problem at all. Both parties might agree on the facts but may still disagree on what should be done about the problem.

Here are some suggestions for understanding the other person's viewpoint. You want to establish that your immediate goal is to understand the other person's perspective, not to solve the problem at this point. Words like "Let me understand this from your perspective" can help. Repeat back what you've heard in your own words: "OK, so correct me if I'm wrong, but what I'm hearing is . . ." and keep going back and forth until the person feels that you understand his or her point of view. You're not AGREEING with them; you're just understanding.

Step 2: Communicating Your Viewpoint

To start this, ask the other person if they are willing to hear your perspective. "Would you be willing to give me a fair hearing in return?" Then, explain how the other person's thoughts and feelings affect you. Again, you want to do this using THEIR communication style. So, if you're not dealing with someone who talks about feelings, describe how it impacts you financially, for example. And make sure that you are clear that your perspective is YOUR experience, not the absolute truth. Ask the other person to repeat back what you just said. You can say, "Just so that we can be sure I expressed myself right, can you tell me how you heard what I just said?" Or, if you're dealing with a visual person you can say, "Can you tell me what that looks like to you?" Again, you're explaining your perspective, but are using their words and language.

Step 3: Separating the Positions from the Problem

This is a key step in negotiating. Here's a visual image that can represent what this step does. In traditional negotiation, you can imagine two people on opposite sides of a big, huge conference table. In the middle of the two is a piece of paper that represents the issue or the problem. Both people are trying to get the piece of paper to their own side of the table. "No, we're going to do it MY way." In Collaborative Persuasion, you both come around to the same side of the table and focus on *solving the problem*! It's not about whose position is better or right. You have to separate that out and identify the actual problem that needs to be solved. So, you might say, "OK, so you and I definitely see some things differently here. I see it this way, and your perception is this. But the fact is, we BOTH want to see this problem solved." You're inviting the other person to the other side of the table, so to speak so that both of you can focus on solving the issue.

The ability to both see the situation from the other person's point of view and then to separate the positions from the problems is one of the most powerful negotiating skills you can possess.

Step 4: Jointly Creating Solutions

Now it's time to brainstorm some solutions to the problem. Ask, "What ideas do you have to solve this problem?" If the solution that they come up with isn't acceptable to you for some reason, then you counter with a suggestion that is fair to both of you. If things start to get heated or emotional, as they often will, take a break. A short break for some water or a walk can cool things down significantly. If the conversation starts to go back to positions of who is right and who is wrong, draw the attention back to the piece of paper in the middle of the table. It's about solving the problem, not being right. Emotions are a powerful energy in a negotiation. Don't be afraid of negative emotions but channel them to the solution instead of letting them derail the negotiation. Statements like "I'm starting to feel frustrated right now. May we take a break?" or "You seem to be getting angry. Do you need a break?" can go a long way to staying on the same side of the table.

Case Study: Dave and Joe

All right. Those are the four steps of Collaborative Persuasion. Let's revisit Dave and Joe and apply the four steps.

- *Step 1*: Understanding the other person's viewpoint. Dave asked Joe how long the car had been on the lot. When he found out that the car had been there for a few weeks, Dave realized that Joe is probably getting pressure from his manager to sell the car. But Dave also saw that the dealership was empty, and the economy has been tough. Joe is still going to need to make some profit on the car.

- *Step 2*: Explaining your viewpoint. Dave explained that he was going to have to spend a considerable amount of money fixing the crack in the dashboard and the paint on the hood. He also explained that it would be tough for him to spend $5,500 on a car with a big crack in the dashboard. Because Joe's communication style is very bottom line-oriented (he IS a sales guy, after all), Dave explained how Joe's position would affect him financially.

- *Step 3*: After finding out how much it would cost to fix the car, Dave goes to Joe and says, "The car needs to be fixed." That is the problem that needed to be solved. Their positions were that Dave wanted to buy the car at a good price, and Joe wanted to sell the car for a price that benefitted him. The problem that needed to be solved was the fixing of the car, so they shifted their focus to solving the problem.

- *Step 4*: Jointly come up with solutions. Dave came up with two suggestions. Either Joe could fix the dashboard and Dave would pay full price, or they could drop the price and Dave could get the dashboard fixed after he bought the car. Joe considered his options and realized that selling the car at a discount would solve his main goals of getting the car off the lot and making the sale. But he still needed to feel like he "won," so he came back with an offer that was $100 less than Dave's suggestion. Dave knew that he could probably get the dashboard fixed for a lot cheaper if he did it on his own, so he accepted the deal. The solution of discounting the car so that Dave could buy it was an effective solution that met both of their needs and solved the problem. That is Collaborative Persuasion at its best!

In our next chapter, we're moving on to the final point on our STARS model, the Skills of the top 2%.

ENTREPRENEUR FOCUS
Mastering Negotiation

Wouldn't it be a different world if everybody thought the way you did? If everybody spontaneously conformed to your every wish, your every thought, your every feeling? Since life doesn't work that way, you would do well to become skilled at the art of negotiation.

In negotiation, after all, neither party holds all the aces. Instead, negotiation proceeds (or should proceed) on a rather level playing field. Since both parties want to win, what is the best way to proceed? Here are five steps.

1. Establish the Relationship

The wise negotiator establishes the relationship before proceeding further. Doing so allows you to get a feeling for the person with whom you are dealing, and vice versa. Though often ignored, "feeling" itself is an essential part of negotiation. So, always be open and sincere. Honesty, integrity, and dignity are palpable qualities and the foundation upon which constructive negotiations are built.

You are best positioned to negotiate when the other party respects you, not only as a businessperson but as a human being. Trust, which is gained through that respect, is the key to successful negotiation.

2. Choose Honey over Vinegar

You'll do better with honey than with vinegar—but the honey must be genuine. Never underestimate the natural ability of other people to sense who you really are. Disingenuous, manipulative, and secretive are feelings that simply cannot be hidden.

When negotiating, you, too, can sense if the other party's values are subpar or lack integrity altogether. No greater red flag exists in the entire arena of negotiation.

3. Focus on the Win-Win

Win-wins are the only way to go. If you approach a negotiation thinking only of yourself, you are a terrible negotiator. Understanding what all parties need and working for all concerned is vital. Keep in mind that seeing things in only black and white (win-lose) creates limited thinking; creativity is essential to good negotiation.

Ultimately, all people involved should find themselves on the same side of the fence. You want to be a player, not a pain. Keep your eye on the big picture and don't get caught up in the small stuff. Stay out of the weeds.

4. Embody Your Inner Adult

Never forget that everyone has an inner adult and an inner child. It is remarkable to witness how even high-level business deals break down because someone at the table starts thinking childishly, instigating that behavior in others. When you see this happening, keep in mind that everyone goes out of balance.

Be the stable anchor, the respectful adult at the table. Helping people come back into balance is often best done by example. Take the high road, embodying your inner adult. Don't argue; instead, understand.

5. Respect the Rhythm of the Relationship

Always remember that there is a rhythm to everything. Don't push it. Oftentimes, it is best to say nothing. Never forget that silent pauses can be a powerful tool. Give yourself and others the time and space to reflect upon everything that has been said.

Don't rush it. Try to sense the natural and appropriate rhythm of all the people at the table, including yourself.

By implementing these five points, you will be well on your way to mastering the art of negotiation. Negotiation is all about relationships. By cultivating and maintaining a good rapport with everyone at the table, every player can win. You're not just creating an agreement; you are cultivating a long-term relationship as well as a reputation.

By mastering the subtle art of negotiation, you establish yourself as a top-rank businessperson, and that in itself may lead to even greater opportunities in the future.

GOAL SCOPING

W e're cruising into the home stretch of our STARS model, as we move on to the final point of the star. We've covered a Sense of Purpose, Traits, Attitudes, and Rapport. Now we're moving on to the skills that the highest-paid, highest-profile people in any industry have mastered.

In this chapter, we're going to cover the first of four skills, which is Goal Setting. You might have learned about setting goals that are SMART (Specific, Measurable, Achievable, Realistic, and Timely).

But is that what the people in the top 2% really do? Or do they have another goal-setting strategy that helps them rise to the top? Putting it another way, if 98% of the people are using one technique and aren't really achieving their goals, wouldn't it make sense to do what the top 2% are doing instead?

There are some flaws in the SMART goal model that go against the goal-setting habits of the top 2%. For example, goals that are Achievable and Realistic are the exact opposite of the kinds of goals that the 2% set. The people who achieve big things—things that redefine their industry—aren't concerned about setting goals that are realistic or achievable. Or, as Albert Einstein said, "You cannot solve a problem from the same consciousness that created it. You must learn to see the world anew." We'll have more on creative problem solving in a later chapter, but you can see that limiting your goals only to those that are realistic or achievable is not going to get you into the top 2%.

What about being specific? That's good, right? Well, yes and no. This, too, can be limiting. Steve Jobs didn't sit down and say, "I want to develop a tablet computer that will sell 3 million in the first 30 days." There's no way he could have known that the iPad would become that popular so quickly. Instead, he probably said to his team, "Let's develop a tablet computer that can reinvent the way people use portable computers." He was specific, but it wasn't tied to numbers.

And even goals that are time related can be a problem. How many times have you set a goal and tied it to a specific time frame and then become disappointed when it didn't happen by that date. "I will lose 20 pounds in six weeks." What happens if you don't lose the weight by that time? That can be very damaging to your sense of competence.

So, while the SMART model is a useful framework in some contexts, it's too limiting in many ways. In order to become one of the highest-paid, highest-profile people in your industry, you're going to need to set higher goals.

GOAL SCOPING

To help you set these kinds of goals, and then to actually MEET those goals, we've developed a process called Goal Scoping. The reason we call our process Goal SCOPING is because the word *scope* has several meanings that are relevant to achieving goals.

One definition of the word scope is a range of view. "I see the entire scope of the project." So it's a broad vision.

But another definition of scope means to narrow that vision down to a target—like on the end of a rifle you have a scope that allows you to focus only on your intended target.

And the word *scope* is also used as a verb that means to figure something out. As in "we're scoping out the problem."

So the term Goal Scoping has many elements that lead to the achievement of a goal: a broad vision, a specific focus, and applied action. Here's an overview of the Goal Scoping system.

In order to successfully make any change, which is really what a goal is—a change from the current situation into a different situation that is better in some way—you need to go through six stages.

First, you need to *identify that a change needs to be made*. We'll get into how that happens in a few minutes. Then, you need to be sufficiently uncomfortable in the current situation to be motivated to make the change. Next you need to *identify what the new reality will look like*. What do you want to achieve by making the change?

Now, the gap from here to there, from the current situation to the new one can be seen as a canyon. You're on one side of the canyon, and you want to get to the other side. How do you do that?

In order to take the risk and endure the discomfort of change, you have to be *convinced that it will be better on the other side*, you have to *know HOW* to get across, and you need the *BELIEF that you can do it*. So it's a combination of pain in where you are, a perceived reward of achieving the goal, knowledge of how to achieve the goal, and a sense of self-efficacy, or the idea that you can do it.

If you have set a goal, and you're not achieving it, it's because one of these elements is missing. Again, the six stages in the Goal Scoping process are:

1. Identify what needs to change.
2. Recognize your pain points.
3. Pinpoint your end goal.

4. Visualize your success.

5. Know what specific actions to take.

6. Believe in yourself.

Let's go through the six stages one at a time.

Identify What Needs to Change

The first one is identifying that a change needs to take place. This takes some time. In *The Structure of Scientific Revolutions* (University of Chicago Press, 2012), Thomas Kuhn describes how change takes place. He's talking about science and history, but the same principles apply to all change. He says that change doesn't happen in a linear fashion. In other words, it's not just a steady improvement day after day. It's more like an explosive leap. Let's use a very basic example—the discovery that the earth was not flat. Many people think that it was Columbus who discovered this, but this is one of the common errors in history.

Anyway, in ancient times, people theorized that the Earth was flat. Each country had its own theory about the nature of the Earth, but based on visual observation, it appeared that the Earth was flat. That was the paradigm at the time.

But then some anomalies to that model started popping up. Seafarers would go out to sea and not fall off the edge. Around 330 B.C. Aristotle said that the Earth was spherical. But it wasn't widely accepted as truth. In the first century B.C., Lucretius said that the Earth couldn't be a sphere because how could people and animals be walking upside down? But by the first century A.D., the paradigm had shifted and most people agreed that the Earth is a sphere. But it took 400 YEARS of disagreement before everyone finally got on board.

And that's how change happens. You're going along with the current state of thinking. This is the way things are. But pretty soon you start noticing anomalies, and you're not so sure that you're right anymore. Soon, more and more anomalies are happening, and you realize that the current paradigm is wrong. And the status quo falls apart. This is a time of change—of confusion—of conflict. Then a bunch of competing theories about what's right pop up. Eventually one of them wins and becomes the new paradigm, and everyone leaps into that new paradigm, and it becomes the status quo—until anomalies start popping up again, and the whole process starts again.

Let's apply this to a more current and personal problem. It's the holidays, and you've gained a few pounds. Your current paradigm of thinking is "Hey, it's the holidays. Everyone gains a few pounds during the holidays. It's not a problem."

But then, you start noticing anomalies to the belief that it's just a few pounds and isn't causing any problems. Your clothes stop fitting. You get winded climbing the stairs. You start needing to take antacids before bed every night. Then, one day, you realize that there is too much evidence to the contrary. Those "few pounds" ARE a problem. You've just finished the first stage of Goal Scoping. You've identified that a change needs to take place.

Recognize Your Pain Points

Stage number two: Sufficient pain or displeasure with the current situation. So, how bad is your current state, REALLY? You see, this is a key reason why people don't achieve their goals. The current situation isn't really bad enough. Maybe you lose those few pounds and stop there. Or maybe you just get used to having the few pounds around. Your tolerance for pain increases.

Sometimes people raise their tolerance for pain instead of eliminating the source of the pain. It's the old parable of how to cook a frog. You just turn the heat up slowly, and the frog won't ever realize that it's being cooked. In life, we get progressively used to the status quo. Until we start noticing anomalies that increase our awareness of the pain. The pain was always there, but you start noticing it more and more. And once it hits a threshold, you finally say, "No more."

I remember a colleague of mine telling me about a turning point she had in her life. This woman was an educated woman with an advanced degree. She got married and had children, and slowly over time, her life started to fall apart. She gained a few pounds with each pregnancy. Her credit cards started filling up. Her marriage became strained. But because these things happened so slowly, she just sort of tolerated it. It became the way things were.

Then, in one month, it all came to a head. She got a pay cut at work because of budget cuts. Her latest diet failed. She had a huge fight with her husband. And then one day, she went to the market to get some items for Christmas dinner for her family, and she had no money. Her checking account was overdrawn, and her credit cards were maxed out. She had to leave the store with nothing. Humiliated, she drove across town in the pouring rain and bought a few items at a different store with the $17 cash she had in her pocket. Walking out of the store, she caught a glimpse of herself in the mirror and had to choke back tears. She got to the car and sat there listening to the rain pound on the car roof. She sobbed and sobbed and then suddenly something changed. Inside, she heard a voice say, "No more. It ends today. I will no longer tolerate this life. I deserve better."

Within six months, she'd gotten out of debt, lost 25 pounds, and had reconnected with her husband. But it took her having sufficient pain to be finally able to do it.

Pinpoint Your End Goal

OK, let's move on to stage number three. Identify what it will look like when the change has been made. The end state. So, in our weight-loss example, this is where you decide what kind of shape you want to get in. You know that you need to change the shape you're already in. But, how healthy do you want to get?

This is the place in our model where you get to choose to think big, or you can choose to be like the other 98%. Using our example, maybe you decide that in addition to losing those holiday pounds, you want to get down to your college weight. Or you might decide that you want to be fit enough to compete in a triathlon. You don't HAVE to set big, out-of-the-box, revolutionary goals. But if you're looking to be one of the highest-paid, highest-profile people in your industry, you're going to need to think about what it would be like if you effected change on a large scale.

The clearer your vision for that end state is, the easier it will be for you to get there. This will help when you get to stage four: assurance that the new state will be better than the current state.

Visualize Your Success

Stage four is where things like visualization, affirmations, goal cards, and the other traditional goal-setting techniques can help. The more often you can remind yourself of how great the new situation will be, the easier the transition will become. So, using our weight-loss example, you might get pictures of yourself when you were a healthier weight and put them on the refrigerator so that you can remind yourself of the better state. You might start saying affirmations. You start doing things to remind you that the future state will be better than the current one.

But here is an important distinction when you're creating a vision for the future. Author and speaker Mike Dooley says, "The details are visualized to *get you excited* about your end results, not to *be* your end results." In other words, we are talking about you having the feeling that the end result will be worth the effort to get there. It's not about creating the specific image in your mind that you're going to exactly have at the end.

Again, going back to Steve Jobs and the iPad. He had no idea what it was going to look like. In fact, they developed another tablet computer early on that doesn't resemble the iPad at all. But I'll bet you anything, Jobs had an image of SOME KIND of tablet computer. And he was able to FEEL how exciting such a device would be.

So, in stage four, you're creating a vision for the end state in order to get yourself to FEEL the feelings, rather than to nail down the details. This is what separates the top 2% from the rest. If you have a goal that's so outside the box that you can't even visualize it, don't worry. Just feel how great it will be to solve whatever problem your goal is trying to solve.

Know What to Do

All right, let's move on to stage five. Knowing what to do. Honestly, this is the easiest part of the whole process. No matter what you can think of, there is someone else on the planet who knows how to do it. You can learn from a role model or mentor, read books, listen to audio programs, take classes, or some other way to learn pretty much anything you need to learn to get from where you are now to where you want to be. So, in our weight-loss example, you might do some research on weight loss or exercise programs. Pretty much, to lose weight, you really do know WHAT to do.

But with some challenges you don't always know what to do. But someone else certainly does. In order to know what to do, find both people who have already solved the problem you want to solve, and find others who are in the same place you are.

Believe in Yourself

And the final stage in the Goal Scoping system is the belief that you can take those actions—self-efficacy. Another way of putting it is your belief about your capability to produce specific levels of performance that exercise an influence of events that affect your life—competence.

According to researcher Albert Bandura, there are four ways you can increase your sense of competence. The first way is through experiences that lead to mastery. You must have some successes in order to believe you can succeed. If you fail too early before you develop a sense of confidence, you won't believe you can ever achieve it.

There are a whole lot of social and societal implications to this idea. But for our goal-setting purposes, it's sufficient to say that the best way to develop a sense of competence is to set yourself up for some small successes along the way.

The second way of strengthening self-beliefs of efficacy is through social models. By doing the right thing, and doing it publicly but without the desire for kudos or fanfare, you can serve as an example to others. Model honorable social behaviors and others will emulate you.

The third way is social persuasion. When other people tell you that they think you can do it, you try hard enough to have some small success, which then increases your belief that you can do it.

The fourth way is mood management. If you're tired, stressed out, hungry, or have something else causing a bad mood, you're less likely to believe you can accomplish your goals. It's amazing what a good night's sleep and a healthy meal can do for your sense of competence.

Ultimately, you need to find a way to believe that you CAN do it. At first, you might find a supportive friend or group. But soon, you start experiencing small successes that lead to mastery. And before you know it, you've achieved your goal!

And that's the process of Goal Scoping. By going through these six stages, you can achieve the goals that will rocket you to the top of your field.

Earl Nightingale could have been describing Goal Scoping when he said, "People with goals succeed because they know where they are going. It's as simple as that."

In our next chapter, we're moving on to the second skill in our STARS model, Time Management.

ENTREPRENEUR FOCUS
How to Make Goals That Will Stick

Here's the sad truth about goals: Not only is quitting an option, but it's also usually the most obvious option.

Obstacles can be so daunting that you really have to commit yourself to believing they can be overcome. If you don't believe that to the core of your being, you will give up when all you can see are the forces working against you. The solutions are rarely obvious, and people often mistake their inability to see the path for there being no path. That's why it's so hard to stay the course and grit it out for the win.

If you are going to succeed, here are the three most critical things you need to do to ensure that your goal improves your life instead of just being something that gets forgotten.

Write Down Your Goals

Goals need to be ridiculously specific. If you don't know exactly what they are, you're not going to be able to build the map of necessary, hyper-specific points of execution.

We can't overstate the importance of making your goals beyond specific and writing them down.

Don't just say you want to win an Academy Award—for which category do you want to win the award? For what type of film? Made by what studio? At what age? What will you wear when you accept the award? Whom will you thank?

The higher the degree of specificity, the easier it is to make a road map to making it come true.

If you know you want to be a character actor and lose yourself in a role, that's one path. If you want to be the lead, that's an entirely different path.

We use the example of an actor because people focus on how much luck goes into getting cast. But if you have enough specificity, you can create your own opportunities.

For proof, read about Sylvester Stallone and how he got the role in *Rocky*. The story will blow you away.

Build a Consistent Routine

Do the most important things in your life before you do anything else. Get the hard things out of the way as soon as possible. This is where we separate the greats from the also-rans. The hard things are called the hard things for a reason.

But if you want to accomplish your goals and not just talk about them, you've got to do the hard things first. Whatever your resolution is, your willingness and ability to do the difficult things will determine your success or failure.

Whether you're on the 50-yard line or the one-yard line, it's all the same—only getting into the end zone counts.

Change Your Behavior by Changing Your Identity

The truth is, you need to feel a massive amount of pride when you follow your routines and get the hard things done—and shame when you don't. If you don't have those emotional rewards and punishments in place, you'll never stick with it.

To oversimplify things, it's about figuring out how to self-congratulate and to really let the sting of disappointment motivate you to do better. It's not about throwing a party when you do one small thing well, and it's definitely not about beating yourself up for something petty either.

It's about finding the perfect balance between delicious carrots and painful sticks. Having said that, learning how to reward and punish yourself well is an art, not a science. A whole book could be written on this topic, and by hook or crook you're going to have to eventually get this right.

CHAPTER

16

POWER PRIORITIZATION

In this chapter, we're moving on to the second skill in our STARS model, Time Management.

It's funny, but we tend to think of time management as a fairly recent concept. We don't imagine that the pioneers with their covered wagons needed to worry much about managing time. "We have to get to California by the weekend, or we'll miss the Gold Rush."

We don't think of the Renaissance masters saying, "OK, I'm going to paint from 9:00 to 12:00 every day, except on weekends." But even though we don't think of it that way, people have been thinking about time and how to use it best for a long, long time.

In a famous speech in 340 B.C. Greek orator Isocrates (not to be confused with the philosopher Socrates) said that successful people are those "who manage well the circumstances which they encounter day by day, and who possess a judgment which is accurate in meeting occasions as they arise and rarely misses the expedient course of action." That's time management.

What's interesting about Isocrates' speech is that it refers to the two different kinds of time that the ancient Greeks understood. They had two different words for the concept of time: *chronos* and *kairos*. *Chronos* refers to the time we're all familiar with—chronological, or clock time. But *kairos* refers to a different kind of time—the right, or opportune moment. And truly successful people, those who are the highest-paid, highest-profile people in their industry know how to manage both.

Imagine it like this. Let's say that every morning you wake up and somebody gives you $24. Every day. You can do anything you want with that $24, but you have to spend it all that day. No rolling it over or saving it. No giving it away.

Everyone else on the planet also gets $24 every day that they have to spend. $24. Every day. The president of the United States gets $24. Scientists working to cure cancer get $24. A prisoner gets $24. Even your slacker brother-in-law who plays video games all day long gets the $24.

But really, $24 can't buy a lot. You can't use it to buy a house or a car. You can't build a skyscraper with $24. So, what do you do with your $24? You can buy 24 things at the dollar store. You could go to the movies and get some snacks.

But is that really all you want to do with your $24? How can you take this finite amount of money and use it well?

That's the difference between the top 2% and everyone else. The most-successful, highest-paid people in every industry have learned to LEVERAGE their $24 into something bigger. They invest that $24 each day into something that can grow bigger and more meaningful.

Of course, we're not talking about actual money here, are we? We are talking about time, and the number of hours that each person is given every day. Whether you're the most successful person in your industry or are a slacker sitting around all day, you still get 24 hours in a day. No more, no less. What makes the difference is how you spend your time. And how you spend your time depends on how you THINK about your time. The STARS actually think about the value of their time differently than everyone else.

We're not talking about someone with an arrogant attitude who believes "my time is more valuable than yours." No, what we're talking about is the understanding that we only get 24 hours in a day, and in order to make the best use of those hours, you need to know what it is that you're good at and focus on doing those things, and either delegate or eliminate the things that aren't a good use of your time.

So how can you develop this skill? How can you learn to think about your time differently? We've developed a system called Power Prioritization that will allow you to shift your thinking about time and how you manage it.

POWER PRIORITIZATION

Power Prioritization is more a way of THINKING about time in the same way that the highest-paid, highest-profile people do. It's not so much about WHAT you do, but WHY and WHEN you do it. Do you see the distinction?

There are seven components to Power Prioritization. You can envision it as an inverted pyramid with seven layers. Going from the top down, starting with the broadest part of the inverted pyramid are the seven components:

1. Values: the things that are important to you
2. Goals: the things you want to change or accomplish in your life
3. Talents: your natural talents and abilities
4. Desires: things you want to spend your time doing
5. You: things that only you can do
6. Others: things that you need other people to help you accomplish
7. Basics: the basic things you need to include in your life

Let's go through them one at a time. To illustrate the components of the system, let's create a person we'll call Sal. Sal is an independent contractor who works on residences building decks and walls and other projects like that. He's married and has one daughter, who plays on her middle school soccer team. He's a religious man and attends church weekly. He also enjoys woodworking and spends his free time crafting furniture in his garage. Let's use him as an example as we walk through the Power Prioritization System.

Values

The first component of the system is Values. The highest-paid, highest-profile people in any industry know that to maximize the impact of your time, you have to use your core personal values as your guide. What is important to you? What are the things that matter to you? Your answers to these questions are likely to be very different than someone else's answers, and that's why, frankly, most generic time management systems don't work. Allow yourself to identify the key values that are the most important to you.

For our example person Sal, he values his relationships with his wife and daughter. He values creative expression. He values spiritual connection. And he values service to others. So, Sal uses those values to guide him as he chooses how to spend his time.

Goals

The second component of the system is Goals. These are the things you want to change or accomplish in your life. What goals do you have?

Sal has a few goals. One, he wants to start selling the furniture that he's making in his garage. Second, he wants to create a wood-crafting workshop that he can lead at the annual church retreat. Personally, he wants to start exercising. And he'd like to spend more one-on-one time with his daughter before she grows up. Those are the goals that need to be incorporated into Sal's Power Prioritization system.

Talents

The next component is Talents. What are the things you are naturally good at? What do you do best? A management consultant once told me, "It's better to maximize your natural talents and abilities so that you can spend your time doing those things instead of trying to get better at the things you don't do as well. No matter how good you get at things you're naturally good at, you'll never be as good as someone who has a natural talent. So, build your life around doing the things you're good at, and delegate or eliminate the things you don't do well."

So, for our friend Sal, he knows that he's good at working with his hands. He's creative and a good leader. He's excellent at engaging with clients, customers, and his fellow church members. He also knows that he's not as good at other things, like managing the finances. He still has to deal with those things, but dealing with them doesn't necessarily mean he has to do it himself. So, his wife runs the books for both the family and the contracting business.

Desire

The fourth component of the Power Prioritization system is Desire. What do you WANT to spend your time doing? Just because you're good at something doesn't mean you want to do it. Maybe you're an excellent cook, and all your friends and family want you to cook every time you all get together. It doesn't mean you have to do it. Similarly, there might be things you LIKE doing that have no relationship to your values or talents. You just like doing them, like watching TV or playing sports. You might be the worst bowler in the world, but if you like doing it, do it! So those are things you need to add in when you're deciding how to think about your time management priorities.

Our friend Sal happens to have a strange ability to clean very, very well. When he does a cleaning project, he's so thorough that even professional cleaners would be put to shame. The thing is Sal hates cleaning. He's good at it, but doesn't enjoy it at all. So, he hires cleaning people. One thing he really DOES love doing is listening to jazz music. He can spend hours just sitting in a comfortable chair listening to old records. Spending time this way is something that Sal really enjoys doing.

You

The fifth component of the Power Prioritization system is You. There are some things that only YOU can do. I have a friend whose husband almost died from an illness, and she said to me, "Dan, I am so thankful he is alive. I could have managed to run our life just fine. I can pay the bills; I can mow the lawn. I can raise the kids. I could be the best mother in the whole world. But there is one thing that I could never EVER be or do no matter how hard I tried. I could never be their father." There are some things in your life that only YOU can do or be. What are those things? What is it that only YOU can do?

Now you have to be careful with your answer to this. Sometimes we use this as an excuse to get overcommitted or focus on the wrong things. How many times have you heard someone say, "Fine, just let me do it. No one else can do it the right way." You have to be careful that you're not wrongly assuming that no one else can do what you think only you can do. A good question to ask is, "If I weren't here to do this, what would happen?" In many cases, the meeting would go on, the brownies would get baked, the job would get done. But there are a few things where you are the only one who can do it. It's your unique presence that defines success in this case. This is a really important distinction to make, because too often we spend our time on things that we THINK only we can do and don't focus on the unique gifts and talents we have to share.

So, for Sal, clearly he is the only father to his daughter. There is no one else who can fill that role. Similarly, the furniture that he crafts is a unique expression of his mind. No one else can do it the exact same way. So, he needs to make sure to spend time on those things that only he can do.

Others

The sixth component of the Power Prioritization system is Others. There are some things that you may want to do, but can't do on your own. You need other people to participate. This is where the idea of leveraging your time comes into play. The highest-paid, highest-profile people understand that they can get more accomplished working with others than they can by themselves. Again, we've only got 24 hours in a day. If you want to accomplish great things, you're going to need to pool your 24 hours with other people.

For Sal, this involves his fellow church members. In order to develop that woodworking workshop, he needs to coordinate with the other people running the retreat. He's got to attend meetings and spend some time communicating with everyone.

Basic Needs

And the last component of the system is the basics. These are the things that everyone needs to include in life. Things like eating, sleeping, grooming, sex, exercise, and the like. They take time, and you've got to put them into your system.

We mentioned that our friend Sal wants to start exercising. If so, then he needs to set aside some time to do that. The time doesn't magically appear; he's got to schedule it in.

MAKING POWER PRIORITIZATION WORK FOR YOU

OK, so now we have the seven components of the Power Prioritization system. How do we apply them to deciding how to manage our daily allotment of 24 hours? Here's what you do:

First you take your values, and you write each one of them in a space on a page. Sal values his relationships with his wife and daughter. He values creative expression. He values spiritual connection. And he values service to others. So, Sal would write down those values on a page, leaving space below them.

Then, you take your goals and you put them under the value they relate to. Remember, Sal wants to start selling the furniture that he's making in his garage. That goes under creative expression. Second, he wants to create a wood-crafting workshop that he can lead at the annual church retreat. That goes under service to others. He wants to start exercising. That goes under his relationships with others because he wants to live long and be healthy for his wife and daughter. But it also goes under service to others because the more energy he has, the more he has to give. So, a goal can go under more than one value. And he'd like to spend more one-on-one time with his daughter before she grows up. That obviously goes under his relationships values.

Next, you make a list of everything that you want to include in your life on a daily or weekly basis. These should ideally be related to your goals and to the things you simply desire to do, as well as the basics that everyone needs to take care of. Also on this list are the things that only you can do. The list is called "Things I Want to Include in My Life."

When our friend Sal did this exercise, these were the things on his list:

- Sleep
- Work
- Exercise
- Time with my wife
- Time with my daughter
- Church
- Woodworking
- Dinner with the family
- Listening to jazz
- Checking personal emails and social media
- Calling my mother once a week

So now he has a list of what he wants to include in his daily and weekly life.

Then, there is another list, called "Things That Need to Get Done, But Not By Me." These are things that you may be good at, but you don't want to do. Also on this list are things that you're not good at and don't want to do.

Sal's list has the following:

- Washing the cars
- Gardening and yardwork
- Finances
- Scheduling appointments
- Going to homeowner's association meetings

So, for everything on this list, you need to delegate or eliminate it. Sal delegates these tasks and eliminates the homeowner's association meetings.

OK, so you've got your list of things you want to include in your life. They cover your values, your goals, your talents, your desires, and the things that only you can do.

Next you create a weekly template that is used for every week; basically, it's a schedule that goes from Monday to Sunday. On it, you write down the reoccurring things, like your work schedule, going to church or synagogue, dinner, meetings, and the like. You're going to schedule a time every day or every week to fit in each one of the things on your list. So, Sal puts in his work, church, time with his daughter, his new golf lessons, etc.

By blocking in every hour of every week, you're able to fit in the things that are important to you. Even if what's important to you is doing nothing, you still have time to do that and get everything else that is important to you done, too. Again, it's not about WHAT you put in your schedule, it's about WHY you're doing what you do, and WHEN.

The last part of the Power Prioritization System is to create a daily schedule based on the weekly template you just created. First thing every morning, or even better, last thing you do at night, you plan the day ahead. By doing this extra step, and not just trying to stick to the weekly template, you're allowing some flexibility. Maybe your kid is sick and can't go to school. Maybe it's a holiday, and you don't have to work but you're going to a party instead. Every day you take the weekly template, and you customize it for the day ahead.

Now, within each day, all you have to do is look at your schedule and see where you are. When you finish one thing, look on the list and see what's next. You're done exercising, now what? It's these moments of transition between one activity and the next where things get off track. You start surfing the internet or chatting on the phone. The next thing you know, you forgot what you're supposed to be doing. But by checking your schedule after every activity, you can remember what you wanted to do and why. If your day has gotten off track, say a meeting ran longer than you anticipated, then you can readjust as needed. Maybe move your workout to a different time or change your dinner plans.

This is what makes the Power Prioritization System so effective. It's fully flexible and customizable. And it allows you to take advantage of those *kairos* moments of opportunity that come up. You're taking daily action to achieve the goals that are consistent with your values. And your life is flexible enough to seize interesting moments when they happen.

There is one other thing to mention: the idea of procrastination. We have more on this topic in a later chapter, but basically there are three reasons why a person procrastinates. They either don't know how to do something, they don't want to do it, or they haven't put it in the right place on their calendar. So, if there's something that you keep procrastinating, take a look at why. Again, we'll get more into this later.

By using the Power Prioritization System, you will learn to think differently about how you spend your time. You'll learn to leverage that 24 hours you are given each day to make the most of your life. That, my friends, is how you think like the STARS.

In the next chapter, we'll move on to the next skill in our STARS model, superior money management.

ENTREPRENEUR FOCUS
Avoiding Priority Pitfalls

Priorities are powerful. Even if you operate at the greatest possible level of productivity, your work won't mean much if it's spent on tasks that have little bearing on the health or development of your company. An entrepreneur's job is to prioritize effectively and ensure that the tasks that demand the most attention get it, but doing that can be difficult in a position so chaotic and unpredictable.

If you find that you consistently have problems prioritizing, or prioritizing the right items, one or more of the following factors might be to blame.

Not Dedicating Time to Prioritize

This is the first mistake, and it's also one of the most common. Prioritizing your tasks and projects requires a dedicated amount of time to complete, just like the tasks and projects themselves. If you don't sit down to clearly prioritize the work on your plate, you'll have no chance of prioritizing effectively—at that point, you're flying blind and hoping your random allocation of tasks will fall in a way that favors your business.

In effect, prioritization should be your first priority; how you accomplish this is up to you. For some, this means taking 15 minutes at the start of your day to evaluate the tasks in front of you and sort them. For others, this is a daily or weekly team meeting to establish goals and directives.

Failing to Consider the Big Picture

The "big picture" can apply in a few different ways. The big picture and bottom line for most projects will come back to making the company profitable in the long term. On a project level, the big picture might be achieving a certain goal or adhering to a set of predetermined standards and expectations.

Every small decision you make within those contexts should be focused on that big picture. Simply put, any project that doesn't make your company more profitable should be a low priority. As a more complex example, within the context of a project with a tight, inflexible deadline, every decision should be made to ensure the fastest possible turnaround.

Getting Distracted by the Little Things

You might have a dozen high-priority items on your list, but if you're bogged down by emails and phone calls all day, you'll never have time to complete them. From one perspective, these little things are distracting you from your top priorities. From another, more objective perspective, these little things are replacing your top priorities as new top priorities.

For the most part, these little things can wait. If you have a project or task that truly demands your attention as the highest priority, set everything else aside. Disconnect from the internet and turn off your phone if you have to.

Not Delegating

Don't get bogged down in work that someone else can handle. Entrepreneurs, especially in small businesses, wear a lot of hats and delve into multiple disciplines, but you shouldn't let an abundance of tasks interfere with you conquering your most important ones. Even if you're the type of person who takes pride in doing as much as possible, this approach often leads to work being completed inefficiently, in an improper order. Know what you do best and demonstrate trust in your employees by delegating work to them.

Refusing to Adapt to New Information

Setting priorities should be somewhat firm; if you changed priorities on a constant basis, your work would be chaotic and inefficient. However, occasionally new information will arise that forces your hand. If you're working on a project to improve your operations, a client emergency can and should take immediate priority.

On the flip side, your highest priority might start as solving a complex, emergency-level dilemma, but if you gain new information that the problem has been solved, you should immediately switch to a different focal point. Keep on your toes and remain as straight as you can while rearranging your agenda when necessary.

Take steps to correct these problems before they creep up to threaten another round of prioritization. Even small priority decisions, like deciding what to work on first during a typical Monday morning, can accumulate and build to bear a significant impact on your eventual productivity. There's no such thing as an absolute "right" or "wrong" decision when it comes to priorities, but each business has unique needs and demands that need to be considered from the top down to be successful.

INTERVAL WEALTH ACCELERATION

I n this chapter, we're moving on to the third skill in our STARS model, Superior Money Management.

Let's start with a story. It's about a guy named Larry, and Larry managed to solve a huge problem in his life. It's a problem that affects millions of Americans, and it might be affecting you, too. See if you can figure out what Larry's problem was by listening to the six principles Larry used to solve his problem.

- *Principle #1*: Larry's problem was a math problem. He was spending more of something than he was bringing in. Once he corrected that imbalance, the problem resolved itself.

- *Principle #2*: The two keys Larry used to solve his problem were planning and tracking. There are a bunch of methods available for Larry to choose from, but they all come down to planning and tracking.
- *Principle #3*: It took some time. Larry's problem didn't happen overnight, and it didn't get corrected right away, either.
- *Principle #4*: Larry's journey wasn't linear. There were ups and downs as well as a few plateaus along the way. Larry had to stay focused on the big picture to stay on track.
- *Principle #5*: There were psychological elements to both the creation of Larry's problem and the solution of Larry's problem. In order to solve the problem, Larry had to address the psychological issues as well.
- *Principle #6*: Even after Larry solved the problem, he needed to keep using the tools he developed. He couldn't return to his old habits, or the problem would come back. It takes daily vigilance to make sure that he doesn't go back to where he came from.

Did you figure out Larry's problem? This is a trick question, because Larry had TWO problems, and he used the six principles to solve BOTH of them. Larry's problems were that he was 35 pounds overweight, and he was also financially broke. He used the six principles to both lose weight and manage his money. Here's how money management and weight management are related.

1. Both weight loss and money management are a math problem. Burning more calories than you take in results in weight loss, while burning fewer calories than you take in results in weight gain. Similarly, spending less than you earn results in money that is leftover for you to choose what to do with it. Spending more than you earn results in debt.
2. Both weight loss and money management require tracking and planning. You need to weigh yourself to measure your progress and plan your weight management strategy. You need to balance your money accounts to see your progress, and you need to plan your money management using a budget. There are many

programs for both weight loss and money management, but they all involve tracking and planning.

3. You can't lose 35 pounds overnight, and you won't get rich overnight. Both things take time.

4. Neither weight loss nor money management is linear. Things happen. The scale goes up and down, and your weight loss can plateau. Life happens, and your finances will go up and down and might plateau for a while.

5. There is a psychological component to both weight management and money management. They revolve around the ideas of valuing yourself enough to invest the time in your own growth and improvement.

6. Even after you lose weight or become wealthy, you still need to use the tools that helped you succeed. If you fall back into the old habits of eating a double cheeseburger for lunch every day or using credit cards for things you can't afford, you'll be back in the same situation again.

So, you can see, there is a strong correlation between weight management and money management. And the same principles of success apply to both.

You may have heard of an exercise strategy called interval training. It's basically where you intersperse short bursts of intense energy with periods of lower intensity training. The results are that you're able to get in shape much, much faster than using regular exercise.

And that's why we've titled this chapter "Interval Wealth Acceleration." Because we're going to apply the principle of interval training to your wealth building, and by doing so, you'll build your wealth much, much faster than if you were to use another strategy.

Are you ready to begin?

ASSESS YOUR FISCAL FITNESS

The first thing you should do is take the FFA, or Fiscal Fitness Assessment. This will help you to determine which interval you should start with. Even if you're more fiscally fit than a beginner, you probably know someone else who's not as fit as you are, and you might pick up some good tips to help them out.

Interval 1: Basic Financial Skills

The first Interval is called Basic Money Skills. Here's an example of someone who is in Interval 1.

Ron is a 35-year-old father of three. He's an hourly employee, and he and his wife rent a home. They've got $11,000 in credit card debt, which is the average amount in America today. They don't have any investments or savings, and they don't have a budget or a regular system for paying their bills. Unfortunately, there's often a lot of month left at the end of their money. Ron takes the Fiscal Fitness Assessment, and it places him in Interval 1.

The goal of Interval 1 is to develop basic money skills. As we learned earlier, there are a lot of great programs out there that can teach basic money management skills, including several programs here at Nightingale-Conant. It's sad to say, but this isn't really something that's taught to us as kids. Too often we just do what our parents did, or even worse, don't do anything at all. Here are some tips and suggestions, though, for some basic money skills development.

TIP #1: You Need to Sit Down and Figure Out How Much Money You're Bringing In and How Much Is Going Out Each Month.

If you're an hourly employee like Ron, sometimes it's hard to know in advance how much money you'll be making. Even still, you need to be able to make an educated guess.

And, if you're not bringing in as much money as you're spending, something in that equation has to change. Remember, this is a math issue. You either need to increase your income or decrease your spending. Or both. The way to increase your income is for someone to get an additional job or develop a passive income stream.

To decrease your expenses, you've got to have some way of tracking them. Go through your bills and figure out how much you're spending to live your life. Yeah, it's a pain to do this, but if you're serious about getting control of your money, you need information.

For example, Suze Orman says that Oprah Winfrey, one of the richest people on the planet, still knows how much she spends each month on her utility bill. Information is power.

So, once you know how much you're spending, you need to make some tough decisions about what to cut back. And this is really a matter of choice. Is it more important to you to have unlimited minutes on your cellphone, or send your kid to karate lessons? It's up to you. Someday you'll be able to afford both, but if you're in Interval 1, today is not that day.

Regardless of what you choose to do, both sides of that equation— income and expenses—need to balance out in Interval 1. We're not talking about debt reduction yet. We're talking about getting in balance.

TIP #2: Clearly You're Going to Need to Develop a Budget.

The words *budget* and *diet* strike fear into the hearts of many. But the fact is, you can't lose weight unless you plan and track how many calories you're eating and using, and you can't manage money without doing the same. A budget is just a fancy way of saying planning and tracking. And your budget is going to change pretty much every month. Some months your kids are in school, and you have those expenses. Other months your kids are on break, and you have different expenses. The holidays are usually only one month, but the budget for that month is very different. You've got birthdays, vacations, and other expenses that occur at different times of the year. You need to plan your budget for each month.

TIP #3: Only Use Cash or Your Debit Cards.

Even checks can be a problem, because you don't know exactly when that money will be taken from your checking account. Instead, set up online bill payment, so you can do it straight from your bank's website, and use cash or a debit card for everything else. Checks and credit cards, or anything else that's going to cause a delay between you spending the money and it coming out of your account, can cause problems.

TIP #4: Keep Track of Any Automatic Debits.

If you're setting up automatic debits from your account, say for a gym membership or something, make a note on your calendar about which day each month the debit is going to happen. This way you won't forget and spend money thinking you have it, and then you get hit with an automatic debit and now you're overdrawn.

TIP #5: Check Your Account Balances Every Day.

Just like you would weigh yourself every day to see where your weight is, you need to take five minutes and check your checking account balance every day. It's just a good habit to keeping on top of things.

The most important thing to understand about Interval 1 is that it's not about tackling credit card debt or even about saving money. It's about developing the core skills that you'll need to manage your wealth when you get it.

Interval 2: Debt Reduction

OK, let's move on to Interval 2. Interval 2 is the debt-reduction phase. Let's go back to Ron.

Ron has now worked through Interval 1. His wife got a part-time job to bring in some extra money, and they eliminated some expenses. Their income and outgo are just about the same. Now it's time to tackle that debt.

Now, different experts will give you different advice on how you should do this. Dave Ramsey says that you should establish a $1,000 emergency fund before you start paying down debts. Personal finance advisor and author John Cummuta says that you don't need to do this, because you'll have some extra cash flow he calls an Accelerator Margin that can be used for emergencies. Whichever way you do it, though, there are two things that pretty much every financial expert agrees on.

One, you completely need to stop using credit cards, for anything, ever. And two, you're going to need to come up with some money for savings. Whether you pay yourself first, or do it after the credit card payments are gone, Interval 2 is about getting rid of your debts and building a little savings.

There is a common misconception among many people who are in Interval 2 about their home mortgage. Many people think that a home mortgage is a different kind of debt than, say, student loans or credit cards. It's the whole "good debt vs. bad debt" argument. These people say, "But I get an income tax deduction on my mortgage. I don't want to lose that!"

Here's the flaw in that logic. If you take out a mortgage, they will charge you interest. It doesn't matter what the interest rate is, they're going to charge you money for the honor of lending it to you. Now, for something huge like a house, most of us aren't able to pay cash for it outright. So, this is a debt that most people are going to have to incur. But to *not* want to pay it off as fast as possible is faulty logic. Because if you're paying more money (because of interest) than the value of what you bought, it doesn't make financial sense. It's like buying a shirt that's worth $10, but you paid $20. The shirt is still only worth $10, but you paid more because you financed it.

Yes, houses can go up in value. But, sadly, a lot of people also learned that houses could go down in value, too. So, let's say you do pay your mortgage debt off and your house rises in value. Great! Now you own something that's worth more than you paid for it. But, if it goes down in value, you don't have to care because you own it outright. You're not still paying on it, and it's only a paper loss if you decide to sell it. Again, looking at a shirt. You bought a shirt for $10, and the shirt goes up in value to $15. That's great because you own it, and now you own something worth more than you paid.

But let's say the shirt goes down in value to $7, Yeah, it's awful that you paid $10 for a shirt that's now only worth $7. But it's only a problem to you if you try and sell the shirt. If you keep the shirt, then it's just a shirt that you bought.

But let's say you didn't pay off your mortgage, and the house increases in value. Great. That's fine. You have more equity in the house, but you're still paying interest on the loan. You're still paying MORE money for the privilege of having borrowed it. Maybe the increase in home value will make up for the interest you will have paid. Maybe not.

It's like if you bought a $10 shirt and financed it and the value of the shirt went up in $15. That's nice, but because you're paying interest, you're still paying $20 for a $15 shirt.

But let's say you didn't pay your mortgage, and the house becomes worth LESS than you bought it for. Now you're in real trouble because you're paying MORE for something that's worth LESS. That doesn't make sense at all. Again using the shirt analogy, you're making payments on a shirt that's worth $7, but your payments are based on the $10 it was worth at the time you bought it. However, because of interest, you're actually going to have paid $20 for the shirt. So, you paid $20 for a shirt that's only worth $7.

Financing is always a bad idea, and it's best to avoid it when you can.

So, the bottom line is that you really do want to pay your mortgage off as fast as you can. You may be getting a tax deduction for it, but if you're not paying interest in the first place, then it won't matter that you're not getting a deduction for it. And you've got the protection you want from fluctuations in the real estate market.

So, you stay in Interval 2 until you are debt free and have a savings account established. Once you're done with this, you're ready to move on to Interval 3: Wealth Building.

Interval 3: Wealth Building

Now, Interval 3 is where people tend to separate into levels. You've got some people who, for them, being wealthy means having a fully funded retirement plan and enough money to take vacations and buy a few toys like a boat or a second home somewhere. For others, being wealthy means having a certain monetary number of net worth. And yet others want to think bigger.

Some of what the wealthiest people on the planet have spoken at length about wealth building. Wealthy people THINK about money differently than nonwealthy people. It's not just that they've accumulated more resources than everyone else. For the people who are the highest-paid, highest-profile people in their industry, they have a different relationship with money than everyone else.

Here are some of the ways that the ultra-wealthy think about money that may be different than the way you think about it.

Mindset #1. Nobody Ever Got Wealthy One Hour at a Time

Remember what we said in the chapter about time management. Everyone only gets 24 hours in a day—no more, and no less. If you are being paid by the hour for your time, you're never going to be wealthy. It doesn't matter if you're the most highly paid hourly earner on the planet. You won't be truly wealthy because there is a limit to the amount of money you can make, and that limit is defined by time.

Now this is great news because it evens the playing field. You have access to the same principles that the people who are making thousands of dollars an hour have access to. It's only a matter of having a different amount of money to play with. But the rules of the game are the same.

The way you build wealth is through the idea of leverage. You can leverage your money through people or investments. Or both. Let's walk through a very basic scenario and revisit our friend Ron. As we said, Ron's wife got a part-time job. We'll call her Julie. Well, they paid off their debts and bought a house and paid that off, too. Now they're in Interval 3 and are ready to build wealth. Ron has become a manager at the company he was working for and is now on salary. Julie quit the part-time job and started a company selling the cookie dough that is her grandmother's recipe. Let's use Ron and Julie to illustrate the two principles of leverage.

Ron uses the power of leverage with money. He takes part of his salary and invests it. Over time, he buys a little real estate, invests in some stocks, and plays around with other investments. He really enjoys it. The principle here is that every dollar he invests is, in essence, given a job. And that dollar goes out to work and comes back with some money that it earned, in the form of interest. So now there are two dollars where there used to be one. Now both of those dollars go out to work and bring in money. And each of those dollars comes back with more money. And so on and so on. This is called compounding.

Albert Einstein once said that the most powerful force in the universe is compound interest. And you can certainly see how that works to your DISADVANTAGE when you're the one paying the interest to your debtors. So why not use that force to your advantage? That's how you leverage money.

But Ron's wife, Julie, is a great illustration of the power of leveraging people. She has a cookie dough business. When she first started out, it was just Julie and her sister Wendy in the kitchen making and packaging cookie dough. They were limited in how much they could produce because it was just the two of them, and they only had so many hours in the day. But eventually, Julie was able to hire people to make the dough. This created more profit. Then she was able to hire even more people to make even more dough. Creating more profit. And so on and so on. So, even though Julie only has 24 hours in a day, she's leveraging the number of other people who only have 24 hours in a day, and they're all pooling their hours together for the same things—making cookie dough.

So, this is the essence of wealth building. Leveraging your money or leveraging the time of other people. Ideally you'll do both.

OK, here is another mindset of the ultra-rich that may be different from the way you're thinking.

Mindset #2: Your Wealth Is Directly Related to the Value of the Service You Provide to Others

But it's not what YOU value, it's what OTHER people value. That is a really important distinction. Think about the difference between teachers and professional athletes. No one is going to question the value that teachers bring to a society. Teachers add tremendous value every day to the lives of the children they teach. However, children aren't the ones with money. Their parents are. So, because children aren't the ones paying the teachers, teachers don't make very much money at all.

Professional athletes, on the other hand, are among the highest-paid people on the planet. What societal value is there in running up and down a court or a field with a ball playing a game? I'll leave that up to you to decide. But the fact is, the people with money, the adults, are more willing to spend their money on the value that professional athletes provide than on the value that teaching children provides. Whether it's morally right or wrong isn't the issue. It's just what IS right now in our society.

Should you choose your career based on what makes the most money? No. Not at all. If your heart is calling you to a career choice that's not one that is highly valued in our society, then do it. But use the leverage idea to get wealthy from another source.

Mindset #3: Value Yourself

The last mindset that we're going to cover in this chapter is a psychological and spiritual one. The highest-paid, highest-profile people in every industry have a certain mindset when it comes to how they value themselves. They believe that they deserve to be wealthy. And they understand that their wealth is a gift that is to be used in service of something greater than themselves. Oprah and Madonna built schools for impoverished children. Bill Gates and Melinda Gates started a foundation. Each of these people has a different way of thinking about money. They see it as a spiritual energy that can be directed to solve a problem that is so big that no one person can solve it alone.

What problem would you like to see solved? Is it homelessness? Hunger? A disease like cancer? You see, it all ties in together. The legacy you leave is tied in to the wealth you have, which is tied in to the relationships you develop, which is affected by the way you manage time. All the points on the STARS model are connected, and at the center of the star is your mindset. Earl Nightingale said it very succinctly when he said, "The amount of money we receive will always be in direct ratio to the demand for what we do; our ability to do it; and the difficulty in replacing us."

In the next chapter, we'll move on to the final skill in our STARS model, creative problem solving.

ENTREPRENEUR FOCUS
Build Your Personal Wealth Habits

When it comes to getting rich, many of us assume it means getting an upscale job with a hefty paycheck. We daydream about how we'll drive a cool car or treat ourselves to fancy dinners out. After all, the more money you earn, the wealthier you are, and then you can do whatever you want, right?

Not quite. Just as important as a well-paying job are the habits that you build when it comes to your budget and finances. How do you spend your money? How much do you save? Are you investing in yourself and your future? And there are even bigger considerations, like how well do you connect with your community, and what kind of impact you are making on those around you.

There are a handful of small but powerful things wealthy people do that set them apart from those who are struggling financially. Start cultivating these habits, and you'll get a sense of what real financial success and independence feels like, as well as what it's like to make a difference.

Create Multiple Streams of Income

It's difficult to become financially independent on one income. If you lose your job, you'll be frantically looking for work while dipping heavily into savings to stay afloat—or, worse yet, you'll be going into debt to pay your bills.

Wealthy people focus on cultivating multiple streams of income so they'll always have something to fall back on during lean times. During boom times, your income will balloon to pad your savings and fund your investments.

You can build passive income, such as from rental properties, stock dividends, or interest from a high-yield bank account. A side hustle is a great way to boost your income while developing a passion or a hobby.

A side hustle could be a business you start on the side, freelancing in an area of expertise, or marketing your skills. Can you teach yoga? Design websites? You can work a part-time job during off hours, or even rent out a room in your home.

The best kind of side hustle is something you enjoy doing, and it's even better if you can create synergy between your different income threads, so they feed into your overarching goals and dreams. If you're able to tap into an area you are passionate about, you'll be determined to persist until you're successful.

Learn to Live on Less

Living beneath your means is the key to creating and maintaining wealth, not to mention avoiding debt. Millionaires know spending less than you earn creates opportunity; you can invest that money, save it, or donate it to a cause or charity you care about. Ideally, you can do all three.

Jim Rohn, entrepreneur, author, and motivational speaker, uses the 70/30 rule as a blueprint for how much to spend, save, invest, and donate. For most people, the difficulty is learning to live on 70 percent of their income after taxes, including spending for all necessities and luxuries. The remaining 30 percent is then broken into 10 percent allocations for investments, savings, and charity.

Living on less than you make requires you to get your spending under control and come up with a budget you stick to. You'll need to learn to be more frugal and to really make your money stretch. It may mean that you drive a used economy car, eat at home more often, or ditch extravagant purchases.

It definitely means that you should stop comparing yourself to others. According to Rohn, "Poor people spend their money and save what's left. Rich people save their money and spend what's left."

When you spend, think about whether this something you really need, or something you just really want.

Make Your Money Work for You

The wealthy invest in themselves. They know the key to making their money work for them consistently over the long haul is creating an investment plan to create wealth. The plan should include regular payments into a mutual fund, a trading account, and retirement accounts.

Accruing wealth also requires making capital investments. This is the money you'll invest in creating an enterprise, such as developing a business, manufacturing a product, marketing and selling your services, or investing in other ventures.

This will require you to take calculated risks while taking into account your long-term financial security. Walking this line require financial savvy. Educate yourself on financial matters. Understand the ins and outs of your investment plan, and make adjustments as needed.

In addition to your investment plan, you should be tucking away at least 10 percent of your paycheck into a "rainy day" savings. It's easiest if you have it automatically deducted from your paycheck. This money is for unexpected expenses and to get you through tough times.

Savings protect your investments. It will keep you from going into debt or needing to pull money from your investments, which, in turn, could cripple your multiple income sources.

Give Back

It may seem counterintuitive to give generously of your time and money, but this is also an important investment. Giving to others and being of service to those who need it most helps you connect with your community and be a part of something bigger than yourself: the greater good.

This is about growing wealth not just in your bank accounts, but in your whole community, which benefits everyone. When you volunteer your time or make donations to causes or issues that your care deeply about, it gives you a sense of joy and purpose.

The idea is to not just be a go-getter, but a go-giver—someone who is focused on others more than themselves. Yes, it's important to stay focused on your goals and be passionate about your dreams. But finding a way to also add value to the lives of other people will benefit you in the long run as well.

Truly wealthy people, the ones who impact society and change our world views, and understand that the more you give, the more those good feelings and vibes come back to you.

MONKEY MANAGEMENT

This chapter will cover the final skill in our STARS model, Creative Problem Solving. By the end of this chapter, you'll have mastered the 18 qualities that differentiate the top 2%, highest-paid, highest-profile people in every industry. You'll be prepared to launch yourself to the STARS.

We placed the chapter on creative problem solving at the very end of the program for a reason. It is the foundational skill that supports your success in each of the other areas. If you're a creative thinker, you'll be able to overcome obstacles to your health, your finances, your relationships, and all the other qualities on the STARS model. And this chapter will give you the tools you need to become a creative problem solver.

THE MONKEY MINDSET

Now, you might be wondering why we titled a chapter about creative problem solving "Monkey Management." In the last chapter we talked about MONEY management. But MONKEY management? What on earth is that?

The monkey is a powerful symbol of several different elements of creativity. A general impression that people have of monkeys is that they are "curious." In addition, the monkey is an important part of Japanese spiritual culture, as they were seen as a mediator between deities and humans. There is a concept in meditation called the Monkey Mind, which is the presence of thoughts that keep jumping around and distracting you. And finally, there's the legend of *The 100th Monkey* (Vision Books, 1982). by Ken Keys Jr., and it goes like this:

The Japanese monkey, *Macaca fuscata*, had been observed in the wild for a period of over 30 years.

In 1952, on the island of Koshima, scientists were providing monkeys with sweet potatoes dropped in the sand. The monkey liked the taste of the raw sweet potatoes, but they found the dirt unpleasant.

An 18-month-old female named Imo found she could solve the problem by washing the potatoes in a nearby stream. She taught this trick to her mother. Her playmates also learned this new way, and they taught their mothers, too.

This cultural innovation was gradually picked up by various monkeys before the eyes of the scientists. Between 1952 and 1958 all the young monkeys learned to wash the sandy sweet potatoes to make them more palatable. Only the adults who imitated their children learned this social improvement. Other adults kept eating the dirty sweet potatoes.

Then something startling took place. In the autumn of 1958, a certain number of Koshima monkeys were washing sweet potatoes— the exact number is not known. Let us suppose that when the sun rose one morning there were 99 monkeys on Koshima Island who had learned to wash their sweet potatoes. Let's further suppose that later that morning, the hundredth monkey learned to wash potatoes.

THEN IT HAPPENED!

By that evening almost everyone in the tribe was washing sweet potatoes before eating them. The added energy of this hundredth monkey somehow created an ideological breakthrough!

But a most surprising thing observed by these scientists was that the habit of washing sweet potatoes then jumped over the sea...Colonies of monkeys on other islands and the mainland troop of monkeys at Takasakiyama began washing their sweet potatoes.

Thus, when a certain critical number achieves an awareness, this new awareness may be communicated from mind to mind.

Although the exact number may vary, this Hundredth Monkey Phenomenon means that when only a limited number of people know of a new way, it may remain the conscious property of these people.

But there is a point at which if only one more person tunes in to a new awareness, a field is strengthened so that this awareness is picked up by almost everyone!

The symbol of the monkey illustrates several important points about creativity and problem solving.

Curiosity

First, the monkey represents the attitude of curiosity. People who are creative problem-solvers approach problems with an attitude of curiosity. "I wonder how we can solve this?" This is in stark contrast to the other 98% of people who see problems as obstacles or setbacks. Walt Disney said, "When you're curious, you find lots of interesting things to do."

So, how can you develop curiosity? Here are five ways you can train yourself to be curious.

1. Ask why. Develop an inquisitive attitude, broaden your perspectives.
2. Ask how. How does it happen? How do we proceed?
3. Ask what if. Speculate, imagine, visualize.
4. Don't accept anything as a "fact."
5. Learn to be curious by always asking questions like why, how, and what if.

The Creative Channel

The next way that the monkey symbolizes creativity is as the Japanese ancients saw the monkey—as a mediator between the deities and the human. This isn't about religion, really. It's about understanding that creativity is about unblocking the lines of communication between you and your source of spiritual inspiration. Creative problem solving is about allowing the inspiration to come THROUGH you rather than FROM you.

So, what can you do if that creative channel is blocked? We've developed a technique called Monkey See, Monkey Do. You might feel a little silly doing this at first, but Nightingale-Conant author Lee Pulos taught this to me, and the benefits outweigh any silliness you may feel at doing this technique. It's based in a technique called EFT. EFT stands for Emotional Freedom Technique and is basically a method for releasing energy blockages in the body's energy system.

You may think of things like chakras and acupressure as kind of nonmainstream. But many realize that it's a valid technique. Deepak Chopra uses it. Madonna uses EFT. So does Nicole Kidman. Singer Michael Ball uses EFT, as does cage fighter Alex Reid. EFT tapping points are basically where the lymph nodes in the body are located, and there is a medical reason why EFT works.

OK, so here's the Monkey See, Monkey Do technique. There is a point on the hand called the karate chop. It's where your hand hits an object if you're karate chopping it. Locate this spot and rub or tap it while saying the following sentence, "Even though I believe I am creatively blocked, I choose to believe that I am connected to the source of infinite creativity."

Then you tap on each of the EFT spots located around the body with some negative beliefs you might have about creativity. Things like, "There's no solution to this problem. It's too big," and "I'm stuck, my creativity is blocked." So, you say these negative beliefs while tapping the EFT points until you feel something open up mentally. It might be a feeling or a thought or a memory. You might suddenly remember your grade school art teacher telling you that you weren't creative.

Then do a positive round. Tap or rub the EFT points and say, "I know that creative ideas are sitting in my mind. I invite them to come out and play. I'm curious to meet the new ideas."

When you're done with the Monkey See, Monkey Do technique, close your eyes, and affirm, "My mind can now solve this problem for me. The solution will come to my mind when I'm not thinking about it." And then stop thinking about it. Let it go. Take a nap, go out to dinner. Whenever your mind starts going back to the problem, release it again. "Nope. My mind is working on that. The answer will come to me." And stay open to inspiration. It might come from a commercial on TV, song lyrics, the name of the guy at the gas station. You've unblocked the channels and divine inspiration can now come to you.

Monkey Mind Mapping

The next way that a monkey symbolizes creativity is through the concept of Monkey Mind. Now, typically in meditation or yoga, Monkey Mind is considered a bad thing. And if you're trying to empty your mind, it is. But as a creative problem-solving technique, it can be very useful. Let's do an exercise called the Monkey Mind Map. It's a brainstorming exercise that helps you use that creative monkey mind to help you solve a problem. Here's how it works. Calm your mind by taking a few deep breaths and centering yourself. You might even want to go outside or in nature.

On a piece of paper, write down a word that represents the problem or block you're facing. Then, look at that word and let your Monkey Mind think of everything to do with that problem. Write down those words. Then, look at each of those words and see what comes to mind. Not every word will lead somewhere, but some might. Also, if you have a random thought, like your grocery list or you think of a person out of the blue, put them on the page as well. If you come up against a block, ask the Monkey Mind a direct question: "What is another way of looking at this?" Then wait and see what the Monkey Mind says.

As with the Monkey See, Monkey Do exercise, you might not hit on a solution right away. You might need to put the Monkey Mind Map aside and think of something else for a while. But soon you'll have a dream or a thought or an idea, and it will be a creative solution to your problem.

Finally, we come to the legend of *The 100th Monkey*. While the book by Ken Keyes Jr. was focused on a specific problem he wanted to change in the world, the ideas within the book can apply to the mindset of the highest-paid, highest-profile people in any industry. Here are some of the messages that the legend of *The 100th Monkey* can teach us about creativity and really about the lessons captured in this entire program:

- It's time we begin to realize that we are far more alike than we are different.
- We are all fellow beings traveling the road of life together.
- We don't live in isolation.
- We are all interconnected.
- We all live in one world.
- We are affected by a lack of harmony of any type anywhere on the planet—even if we're not consciously aware of it.
- We are not separate.
- What we say and do can affects the well-being of all of us.
- We know that our health may be affected if we live among diseased people.
- What we are beginning to learn is that our peace of mind may be affected if we live among disturbed people.
- Our happiness may be affected if we live among unhappy people.
- Our love may be affected if we live among clashing, unloving people.
- Let us challenge our present approaches and rethink old assumptions.
- It takes a strong person to be able to communicate lovingly but directly what he or she wants to someone who disagrees—and acts hostile.
- You will increase your skill in helping the world when you learn to be mentally flexible.

- This means being able to constantly blend back into creating an experience of life as a whole with appreciation, cooperativeness, and love for the people around you—even when they oppose you.
- Any problem created by the human mind can be solved by the human mind.

By tuning into the new awareness that is held by the top 2%, you might be the 100th monkey. You might be the final tipping point that raises awareness for everyone. And THAT is a star worth shooting for.

ENTREPRENEUR FOCUS
Lean into Your Unique Problem-Solving Skills

Problem solving is one of the most important aspects of entrepreneurship. As both the founder of your organization and the leader of your team, you'll be responsible for identifying and solving the problems of your customers, partners, employees, and your company, in general.

The question might be posed as to whether successful entrepreneur problem-solvers use their natural talents to find success, or whether those skills are cultivated after years of experience. But, either way, I would maintain that successful entrepreneurs think about and solve problems differently from most other professionals.

How is this problem-solving process distinctive, and how can you apply that difference to your own work habits? And what's different about entrepreneurs-as-problem-solvers in the first place? Here are six ways:

1. They Identify Problems First

Some people think of entrepreneurial types of as creative inventors; given a blank canvas, they can come up with a product that people will love. But that's not usually the case. Instead, the most successful entrepreneurs are those who first identify a key problem in the market, then work to solve that problem.

Airbnb, for example, started when its two founders, Brian Chesky and Joe Gebbia, realized that two problems existed in the same business area; one, they were having trouble affording rent in New York; and two nearly all the hotel rooms in the city were consistently booked. Those founders didn't come up with their idea out of thin air; they recognized two key problems and devised a solution to solve both simultaneously.

2. They Stay Calm

According to a study by TalentSmart, 90 percent of top performers are able to manage their emotions successfully when they experience high levels of stress. This isn't a coincidence: When you allow your emotions to get the better of you when facing a problem, you subject yourself to reactive decision making, and lose touch with your logical side. Accordingly, you make poorer decisions, and in some cases, may look bad in front of your employees.

Of course, "staying calm" when you face a major issue is, itself, a major issue. It takes years of practice and self-discipline to learn how to prevent your emotions from taking over. You need the kind of perspective that only high-stress experiences can give you. That perspective? No problem, by itself, is unconquerable or incapable of being solved through alternative approaches.

3. They Start with the General and Work toward the Specific

When addressing a problem, most people get caught up in the details, but successful entrepreneur-strategists tend to think about problems more generally before working down to the specific details. For example, if entrepreneurs' cars break down on the side of the road, they aren't immediately concerned with the peculiarities of the engine that led to its malfunction; instead, they recognize that the car isn't drivable and work to get it to the shoulder—and safety.

This approach helps you see the high-level nature (and consequences) of your current problem, giving you a reliable context for solving it.

4. They Adapt

Successful entrepreneurs are also willing to adapt to solve a problem; they aren't beholden to the image, processes, or lines of thinking that got them into the problem in the first place.

For example, Nokia—probably best known as the top cell phone provider in the world between 1998 and 2012—started out as a paper company that later transitioned to producing rubber tires and galoshes (as the needs of its customers changed). When the demand rose for military and emergency service radio phones, Nokia transitioned again and started making those devices, eventually selling off its paper and rubber divisions.

In short, faced with changing available resources, market demand and competition, Nokia reinvented itself rather than remaining stagnant or applying old rubrics to new problems.

5. They Delegate and Distribute

Entrepreneurs also know they aren't the most effective problem-solvers on their own; instead, most problems are best handed over to specialists who better understand those problems. Accordingly, when an entrepreneur faces a tough decision or a difficult situation, he or she typically delegates the judgment needed to an expert and calls in help to carry out that expert's solution as efficiently as possible.

Entrepreneurs also aren't afraid to delegate authority to the internal hires they trust and aren't hesitant to spend money on external firms and consultants if that solution will solve the problem faster and more efficiently.

6. They Measure Outcomes and Reflect

Successful entrepreneurs actually do more than just solve the problem. After applying a fix, they spend time measuring the results of their efforts with analytics tools and reflecting on those outcomes. Learning from the approach they've chosen, whether it turns out to be a success or failure, is what equips them to make even better decisions in the future.

So, if you aren't an entrepreneur in your own right, there's much you can gain from adopting the problem-solving tactics of someone who is—someone who's a success at both entrepreneurship and decision making.

Applying different modes of thinking and new leadership styles and being open to more potential problem-solving options are the strategies that will help you solve problems more thoroughly and reap better long-term results.

RESOURCES
(In Order of Appearance)

The Entrepreneur Focus sections in this book are derived from the following articles, which can be found at www.entrepreneur.com:

Charley Harary, Entrepreneur contributor. "Want to Find Your Purpose? Stop Looking for It. Start Living With It." Entrepreneur, February 4, 2016. https://www.entrepreneur.com/article/254924.

Moe Kittaneh, Entrepreneur contributor. "The Real Person's Guide to Finding Your Passion and Loving What You Do." Entrepreneur, December 2, 2014. https://www.entrepreneur.com/article/240303

Steve Sponseller. Entrepreneur contributor. "How to Recognize Business Inflection Points and Innovate to Survive Them." Entrepreneur, June 9, 2016. https://www.entrepreneur.com/article/275816

Sherrie Campbell. Entrepreneur contributor. "12 Ways to Stop Undermining Your Self-Esteem." Entrepreneur, November 12, 2015. https://www.entrepreneur.com/article/252747

Deep Patel, Entrepreneur Leadership Network VIP. "14 Effective Ways for Entrepreneurs to Boost Their Energy Throughout the Day." Entrepreneur, September 17, 2018. https://www.entrepreneur.com/article/319788

Jennifer Spencer, Entrepreneur Leadership Network VIP. "6 Ways to Grow Your Business by Focusing on Personal Health." Entrepreneur, May 4, 2020. https://www.entrepreneur.com/article/349104

Aytekin Tank, Entrepreneur Leadership Network VIP. "Don't Learn More, Learn Smarter. A Quick Guide to Agile Learning." Entrepreneur, November 8, 2019. https://www.entrepreneur.com/article/341618

Tor Constantino, Entrepreneur Leadership Network contributor. "5 Essentials for Switching from Pursuit of Happiness to Just Being Happy." Entrepreneur, April 21, 2016. https://www.entrepreneur.com/article/274414

Nina Zipkin, Entrepreneur staff. "Follow These 8 Steps to Stay Focused and Reach Your Goals." Entrepreneur, October 23, 2017. https://www.entrepreneur.com/article/288682

Rashan Dixon, Entrepreneur Leadership Network contributor. "5 Factors for Planning Your Entrepreneurial Legacy." Entrepreneur, April 16, 2020. https://www.entrepreneur.com/article/349179

Deep Patel, Entrepreneur Leadership Network VIP. "14 Proven Ways to Improve Your Communication Skills." Entrepreneur, May 15, 2019. https://www.entrepreneur.com/article/300466

Jeffrey Hayzlett, Entrepreneur contributor. "4 Principles of Servant Leadership." Entrepreneur, October 16, 2019. https://www.entrepreneur.com/article/340791

Sameer Somal, Entrepreneur contributor. "The New Networking: 8 Strategies for Building Real Relationships." Entrepreneur, August 27, 2018. https://www.entrepreneur.com/article/318453

Michael Mamas, Entrepreneur contributor. "5 Steps to Master the Art of Negotiation." Entrepreneur, December 11, 2015. https://www.entrepreneur.com/article/253074

Tom Bilyeu, Entrepreneur contributor. "How to Make Goals That Will Stick and Help You Thrive." Entrepreneur, May 9, 2018. https://www.entrepreneur.com/article/312622

Anna Johansson, Entrepreneur Leadership Network writer. "5 Mistakes That Make Effective Prioritizing Impossible." Entrepreneur, November 11, 2015. https://www.entrepreneur.com/article/251713

Deep Patel, Entrepreneur Leadership Network VIP. "4 Money Habits That Separate Building Wealth from Just Making a Living." Entrepreneur, June 16, 2017. https://www.entrepreneur.com/article/295024

Entrepreneur staff. "Entrepreneurs Solve Problems Differently Than Other Professionals. Really! Here Are the 6 Ways." Entrepreneur, October 30, 2017. https://www.entrepreneur.com/article/303407

ABOUT
THE AUTHOR

Nightingale-Conant is the world leader in personal development, spiritual growth, wealth building, mind development, and wellness content. The company provides audiobooks, courses, seminars, and videos from notable authors like Brian Tracy, Jack Canfield, Deepak Chopra, Jim Rohn, and Zig Ziglar among many others. Access the full catalog at www.nightingale.com.

INDEX

CPSIA information can be obtained
at www.ICGtesting.com
Printed in the USA
JSHW020314150821
17855JS00003B/3